WOMANSTYLE

BY LEAH FELDON

Design by Betty Binns/Drawings by June Reynard

WOMANSTYLE

YOUR PERSONAL GUIDE TO TIMELESS FASHION

CLARKSON N. POTTER, INC./*Publishers*

DISTRIBUTED BY CROWN PUBLISHERS, INC., NEW YORK

To my mother and father, Henrietta and Paul Kahan.

PHOTO CREDITS
Neal Barr: front and back cover. Barbara Bordnick: copyright © 1977, pp. 78, 90. Alex Chatelain: pp. 62 (*top left*), 83, 85 (*center right*), 132. Guido Chigani: pp. 27 (*right*), 102 (*bottom*), 108. Patrick Demarchelier: copyright © 1978 by the Conde Nast Publications Inc., p. 41. Arthur Elgort, copyright © by the Conde Nast Publications Inc., 1978, p. 53, 1979, p. 122. Robert Farber: p. 73, 119 (*right*). Al Freni: pp. 19, 72. Leah Feldon: p. 113. Ray Garcia: pp. 14, 15, 62 (*center*), 101, 102, 105, 144, 147. Gary Gross: p. 114. Horst: p. 58. George Hurrell: p. 124. (Photograph of Marlene Dietrich from the book *The Hurrell Style*, text by Whitney Stine, T.Y. Crowell, 1976-77). Klaus Lucka: p. 118 (*right*). Jacques Malignon: pp. 50, 60, 63, 65, 71, 74, 82, 85 (*bottom*), 92, 104, 105 (*bottom*), 106, 130, 151 (*bottom*). Hans Pelgrom: pp. 18, 22, 23, 25 (*right & bottom*), 33, 47 (*right*), 51, 66 (*top*), 94 (*bottom*), 116, 118 (*left & center*), 133. Mike Reinhardt: p. 52. Alberto Rizzo: pp. 25 (*top*), 34, 36, 44, 45 (*bottom left*), 46, 68, 80, 93, 94 (*top left*), 126, 128. Steen Svensson: pp. 38 (*right*), for Trevira: 62 (*bottom*), 83, 86 (*left*), 149. Charles Tracy: pp. 56, 64, 81, 117, 125, 127, 153. Bernard Vidal: pp. 54, 85 (*top right*), 119 (*left*), 129. Albert Watson: pp. 10, 31 (*right*), 37, 43, 45 (*top left & bottom*), 66 (*bottom*), 70, 85 (*center right*), 87, 94 (*center*), 96, 97, 102 (*top*), 103, 120. Butterick Marketing Company: p. 20 (*bottom*), 25 (*center*), 26 (*left*), 30, 31 (*left*), 32 (*left*), 35, 39, 42, 47, 62 (*top right*), 94 (*top right*), 95, 140, 151, 152.

Library of Congress Cataloging in Publication Data

Feldon, Leah, 1944–
    Womanstyle: your personal guide to timeless fashion.

    Includes index.
    1. Clothing and dress.   2. Fashion.   I. Title.
TT507.F44   646'.34   79-9086
ISBN 0-517-53871-7

Printed in the United States of America
Published simultaneously in Canada by
General Publishing Company Limited

CONTENTS

PREFACE

- What should I wear?
- What exactly is appropriate for a specific occasion?
- Which of the many styles available is best suited to my type of body?
- How do I recognize the subtleties of my body proportions?
- What colors and textures are best for me?
- How do I determine my most flattering hemline?
- How can I use accessories to my advantage?
- How important is my personality in determining my best style?
- How can I put together a good-looking, practical wardrobe?

If you have ever asked yourself any of these questions, you are probably very much like the rest of us. You are looking for some guidance but uncertain of which way to turn. With so many options, so many styles of dress available that are appropriate to our needs, finding the right style—the one that is best suited to our bodies and our personalities—can be downright confusing.

Womanstyle will answer these questions and many more—not just in general, but with you and your specific body type in mind. It will take you step by step from an elementary understanding of your individual body proportions and why certain clothing shapes and lines are better for you than others, to a sophisticated strategy and range of fashion ideas for planning the perfect wardrobe for your body, your personality, and your life-style. And throughout the book you will have the added benefit of the advice and thoughts of some of the top professionals in the fashion and beauty business.

I first decided to write *Womanstyle* when I became aware of the confusion that women seemed to be feeling about fashion. I have overheard people on buses, in restaurants, and even at elegant gatherings expressing doubts about which way to go with fashion. I have been asked by strangers in department stores, as an objective third party, what I thought of a particular outfit. I have watched friends having a hard time making what should have been simple fashion decisions and listened to their complaints about the mistakes they have made. Not too long ago one of these friends asked my opinion of some things she'd bought in a chic boutique in Greenwich Village. The clothes were great, I told her, but they did not quite suit her: the shirts were too bright and loud for her coloring and personality, the scarves were too bulky for her small frame, and the cut of the pants didn't do her figure justice. In a word, they seemed like someone else's clothes. She said that she had had the uneasy feeling that they weren't right for her but that Maurizio, the dapper, silver-tongued boutique owner, had convinced her that they were "very today" and looked wonderful, despite her instinctive reservations. Playing on her insecurities, Maurizio had done a smooth bit of selling.

Giving basic information, hints, and tips to solve fashion problems has been my business for more than ten years. In 1968 I began work as a stylist for a top New York fashion photographer whose clients included *Harper's Bazaar* as well as major advertising accounts. His photography studio was a perfect training ground for my initiation into the fashion business. I was constantly surrounded by the best in the profession—models, designers, editors, and art directors.

After three years of learning the business, I decided to strike out on my own. As a free-lance stylist, I am hired by various advertising agencies and photographers for specific assignments. Single ads, total advertising campaigns, and television commercials constitute the major part of my work, although I have been employed on several industrial films as well. No two assignments are the same; each job varies according to the needs of the client. But, in general, I help determine the feeling and mood of the ad, select the proper model or models (casting), and pull together the perfect clothes and accessories.

What I do as a fashion stylist is make the same kind of decisions many times a day that you do when you are buying an outfit. Because of my many years of experience, I can now pull together an eye-catching outfit for myself or a job in two minutes flat, with hardly a second thought. But I have to admit it wasn't always so easy, and I can sympathize with and understand the frustrations and doubts a person with no such experience faces when confronted with an endless array of inviting clothes.

My first styling job was a mildly traumatic experience. We were photographing a yellow raincoat for a *New York Times Magazine* ad. Although I had to select only a few minor accessories—jewelry, hat, scarf, gloves—the decisions seemed monumental at the time. I was nervous and jittery for two days before the shooting as visions of possible color combinations and scarf choices whirled around in my poor head. To my great relief, the brown shoes, Pucci scarf, and brown knit cap I chose were a great success. I passed my yellow raincoat test with high praise from a very patient boss and after only a few sleepless nights. Fortunately, for me and my clients, the decisions came faster and became easier with every job I did. Now, these decisions are swift and disciplined.

The longer I've worked in styling the more finely tuned and trained my eye has become. And the more I dress other people, the more I realize that their style, that is, their personalities, their aura, and their movements greatly influence the way clothes look on them. I've learned that there are two reasons that fashion works: (1) The knowledge and application of the basic fashion principles of proportion, line, color, and texture; (2) the personal style of the wearer.

There must be a harmonious blend of the two. And that's what this book is all about. I'm going to show you just how easy it can become.

During my years in the business, I've

worked with actresses, actors, top models, designers, and celebrities. I've run the gamut from Cheryl Tiegs to Joe Namath to your local Avon lady. A great part of the fun of doing what I do has been the people, many of whom have become good friends of mine. They have generously offered their assistance on this book, and their ideas, comments, and suggestions, I know, will be invaluable to you.

I hope that by the time you've finished reading this book you will no longer fear fashion and suffer doubts and confusion about it. *Womanstyle* will give you the confidence to enjoy fashion and the boldness to create your own. No more worrying, Am I overdressed? Am I underdressed? Am I wearing the right thing? No more worrying because *you* will know how to dress for *you*.

ACKNOWLEDGMENTS

Many, many thanks to the fashion pros who generously contributed their time, thoughts, and talents to the making of *WomanStyle*:

To photographers Horst, George Hurrell, Ara Gallant, Arthur Elgort, Patrick Demarchelier, Mike Reinhardt, Alex Chatelain, Guido Chigani, Klaus Lucka, Al Freni, Scavullo, Barbara Bordnick, Jacques Malignon, Gary Gross, Bernard Vidal, Robert Farber, Steen Svensson. And very special thanks to cover photographer Neal Barr, who initiated my fashion career and who has been a terrific friend from the very beginning; my "soulbrother," Ray Garcia, who was always there (with or without his camera) whenever I needed help and encouragement; Charles Tracy, whose good karma and enthusiasm has always served as inspiration; Albert Watson and Hans Pelgrom, who were kind and generous beyond the call of duty; Alberto Rizzo, whose friendship and ideas, as well as his photographs, contributed greatly to the book; and to Judy Lane, Elizabeth Watson, Andrea Fonyo, and Martine Julien, the "right arms" of their respective photographers, each of whom went out of their way to lend a needed hand.

To the models and actresses whose personal insights and individual styles are an integral part of this book— Kim Bassinger, Susan Blakeley, Suzy Chaffee, Alva Chinn, Susie Coeleho, Debbie Dickenson, Janice Dickenson, Barbara Feldon, Erin Grey, Yasmine, Jerry Hall, Susan Forrestal, Susi Gilder, Jane Hitchcock, Anne Holbrook, Beverly Johnson, Pat McGuire, Margrit Ramme, Pam Suthern, Michelle Stevens.

With extra special thanks to Maud Adams for being interview number one; to Sue Smith, Pat Cleveland, and Molly Schotz for donating their talents and after-work hours for specific photographs; and to my close friends Bethann Hardison, Shelley Smith, and Betsy Cameron for being helpful, comforting, and loving.

To the designers who contributed their expertise—Bill Blass, Stephen Burrows, Perry Ellis, Betsy Gonzales, Calvin Klein, Mary McFadden, Fernando Sanchez, Joan Sibley, and Willi Smith.

To the fashion experts behind the scenes who make the whole thing fit together—Nina Blanchard, Johnny Casablancas, Eileen Ford, Phyllis Posnick, Polly Mellen, Eugenia Sheppard, Diane Smith, Beverly Silver, Diana Vreeland, Wilhelmina, Zoli, Nancy Evans, Ina Kahn, David O'Grady, Monique Pillard, Kathy Travis, Laurie Mallet, Helen Murray, Susan Hunter, Diana Shiel, Ed Pulinsky, Cindy Burks, and Abby Siegl.

Much gratitude to my business pals—makeup artist Way Bandy and hairstylists Suga and Martin Downey, who helped fill in the empty spaces.

Much appreciation to the companies and stores that allowed use of their advertising photos: Ann Taylor, Bergdorf Goodman, Conde Nast Publications, Inc., Garfinkel's, Hoechst Fibers (Trevira—in-house agency), Moygashel Linen, Saks Fifth Avenue, and Vogue Patterns.

And very special thanks to those who were totally supportive throughout—my sister, Deborah Kahan, who personally tested all my proportion experiments; my close friends Perri Chasin, Isaac Berger, and Peter Morrison; my agent, Connie Clausen, and my publisher, Jane West, who had faith before the proof was actually in the pudding; Betty Binns and June Reynard, for their wonderful design and illustrations and their unflagging energy and patience. To my editor and faithful ally, Nancy Novogrod, for her invaluable assistance, and to Ellen Gilbert, who gave us both excellent help; to Mike Fragnito and Pam Pollack for their tireless efforts in producing *WomanStyle*. And finally to Nancy Kahan and Betsy Nolan for their efforts that have just begun.

BODY THINKING

BEST BETS FOR YOUR PROPORTIONS

Of all basic fashion principles, proportion is the most important. Without a doubt, it is the most subtle. According to Webster, proportion is "a relationship between quantities, such that if one varies the other varies in a manner dependent on the first." Translated loosely in terms of fashion: if you make your legs look longer, your torso will look shorter. Webster continues, proportion is "a harmonious relationship . . . balance and symmetry." Translated again for our purpose: if the proportion of your clothes is not in harmony with the proportions of your body, you will never look terrific. You may not look awful, you may even look rather good, but you will not look the best you can. Looking your best may require a new wardrobe, or may simply require minor alterations to the clothes you already own. If the answer is as simple as nips and tucks, then you have everything to gain and nothing to lose.

Basically, proportion is easy to understand, once your eye is used to seeing it. If you've ever had the feeling that your clothes are tasteful, but they don't do anything for you, it might just be a matter of proportion.

THE PERFECTLY PROPORTIONED BODY AND THE OTHER 90 PERCENT

The female body comes in innumerable shapes and sizes—it is never just a question of being tall or short or fat or skinny. Proportion, and the many possible combinations it

The perfectly Proportioned body

Keep your body in as good a condition as possible. That doesn't mean you have to be rail thin, but it does mean you have to be fit . . . walking well is vital. Vitality and relaxation of the body—relaxation when you sit down, vitality when you move about. I think that's very important for clothes.
DIANA VREELAND

allows, is the factor that most strongly affects the way a body looks. This is what is termed a perfectly proportioned body

It is known in the fashion business as "a perfect $2.98 body," i.e., a body so perfectly proportioned that anything, even a cheaply made, poorly designed, unattractive item retailing for $2.98 will look good on it.

While the perfectly proportioned body will never go out of style, the clothing of today is specifically geared to another enviable body type—the clothes rack (my pet name for the tall, lanky model's body). No wonder that many of us feel left out by high fashion when the leading designers proportion their garments on models who are 5 feet 8 inches or 5 feet 9 inches tall and magazines such as *Vogue* and *Bazaar* display them on these elongated, narrow bodies.

But don't be distressed if you're neither perfect nor have that lean and hungry look. I

assure you that very few women are ideally proportioned—less than 10 percent. Chances are that like me and the other 90 percent of the total female population you have got a problem or two. That's why it is of the utmost importance that you understand which shapes and lines will enhance *your individual body type* and which ones will not. No matter what your height or bone structure, being aware of *your specific proportions* will enable you to find the clothes that will make you look as good as that privileged and elite 10 percent. You simply need to learn how to make certain allowances. Hence this quick but obligatory warning: *to fully understand your proportions and to deal with them effectively, you must be able to look at yourself and assess your flaws.* Understand your imperfections and do not be overcritical. And never, never indulge in

Proportion is something that happens in your eye, rather than with a measuring tape. It's a balance of color, texture, and the direction in which your eye goes.
JOAN SIBLEY

dreams of what might have been. Such worthless thoughts as "If I were only two inches taller, I would look great" are a waste of time, as well as a huge energy drain. Work with what you've got and make it look spectacular.

On the other hand, don't cop out. If you feel you are 15 pounds overweight, make a positive decision to pare yourself down to fighting form. A firm, healthy body will make you feel better, look better in your clothes, and will help you project a positive attitude about yourself. Ara Gallant, a leading hairstylist and fashion photographer who has worked with numerous celebrities and models, sums it up this way:

> Attitude has a lot to do with the way people look. I've seen the most beautiful women look unattractive because of their attitude. Women who are secure and confident, however, have a special aura that transcends traditional beauty. All women are potentially terrific—they just have to believe in themselves.

If it is in your plans to lose a few pounds, keep in mind that it's important to look good while you're getting in shape. Too many women (and men, too, for that matter) get caught in a vicious circle. They know that they are overweight, so they decide to wait until they lose a few pounds to buy any new clothes. Intellectually it makes sense, and economically as well. But the catch is that if the clothes you already own are too tight and you feel you don't look good, you tend to hide out at home. You don't go out as much because you have nothing to wear. You stay in, watch TV, get a little bored or depressed, and all of a sudden you feel the urge to have a little something to eat. It's understandable, but don't let yourself get ensnared in this all too common trap.

One other thing you're going to need, aside from your iron will, is a good-quality full-length mirror—one of life's absolute necessities. There is simply no way to truly see proportion without it. So if you don't have one, turn to

"Mirrors" in your Yellow Pages, do some comparison shopping, and have one delivered. It is important that the mirror be of very good quality, because an inferior quality mirror will distort your image. Although you might get a warm, tingling sensation inside every time you see an unusually slender you passing before your distorted mirror, it is not reality. And heaven forbid you should have the misfortune to acquire a mirror that turns your lovely shape into a squashed tomato. *A good-quality full-length mirror is a must.*

LINE

Line is your basic fashion silhouette. It is the way your clothes appear to divide your body. The hem*line,* for instance, visually determines the length of the leg in proportion to the rest of the body. The waist*line* appears to separate the upper portion of the body from the lower. The neck*line* visually sets off the neck and head from the rest of the body.

Since your line (or fashion silhouette) is determined by your choice of clothes—their style, color, shape, texture, and bulk—you must get to know the best line for your body and how to choose the clothes that will create this line.

To facilitate what may at first seem like a Herculean task, think of the body as a whole—the whole being equal to the sum of its parts. One portion of the body will appear to change in direct ratio to the others; thus, if you accentuate one part of your body, another will assume less importance.

If one part of your body is out of proportion to another, you can correct this through the lines of your clothes. They can create the illusion of a perfect figure.

That is what you must now set about to do: find the lines that create this illusion.

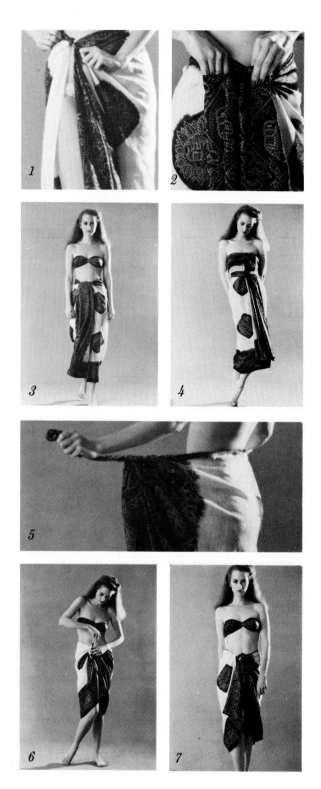

How to wrap a sarong:
Tie a length of fabric around your waist (1), fold the excess in accordion pleats (2), and tuck the pleats into the skirt (3). This sarong can also be wrapped and worn about the bust (4). For another style of wrap, twist the ends of the fabric (5), bring them together, then twist until they curl into a knot (6). The sarong (7) is neat and comfortable and easy to make.

Getting to know your body (or the one-sided dress caper)

Here is a terrific experiment you can do by yourself at home that will help you determine the hemlines and waistlines that are best for you. It will make some of the subtleties of proportion and line crystal clear. You will need:

1. A good-quality full-length mirror.

2. Two-and-a-half yards of a middle-weight summer cotton fabric in a beautifully colored print that will look sensational with a summer tan. (Most fabric comes in a 36-inch width.) If you buy a piece of fabric that you love, then you can "wrap it" and wear it as a sarong, suitable for beach or home (see pictures for wrap instructions). And, if you decide one day not to sarong it, you can always use it as an emergency beach blanket.

3. A wide belt and a medium-width belt. If these are not at your disposal, use a long scarf, making it into various widths as you wrap it around your waist.

4. At least two pairs of shoes, each with different heel heights (the ones you usually wear).

This easy experiment will help you determine your best lines.

Here's how the experiment works:

☐ Take your fabric, your relatively unclothed body (socks prohibited), and your shoes and belts over to your full-length mirror. (1)

☐ Shake out the fabric lengthwise, take the top corners and twist them a bit, and holding the material in front of you, tie the twisted corners around your neck. (Forget the fact that your back is bare—it's of no consequence to this experiment.) (2)

☐ Tuck the sides of the fabric that are over your bosom under a bit, creating a kind of cowled neck, halter-style dress. (3)

☐ Put on one of the belts and the shoes. (4)

☐ You are now standing in a colorful, beautifully patterned, full-length, one-sided dress. (5)

☐ Raise the hemline gradually; neatly draw the excess fabric under the belt and then pull it up, making the top of the dress somewhat blouson. Changing the length of your hem will probably change the appearance of your legs—they will look thicker or narrower depending on where the hemline falls. Which length makes your legs look best? Some of you will find several lengths that work for your legs, others will find only one or two. These are *your* hemlines. (6)

☐ Keep the fabric situated at the hemline, or hemlines, best suited to you. Blouse the top so the waistline is made to appear long. To see what a high-waisted look will do for your proportions, take the extra bloused fabric and tuck it gracefully under the belt, gently pulling the excess toward the back to get rid of as much bulk as possible. Play around. Change the lines of your "new dress"—high, low, medium waistline, blouson. Change the belts and shoes, and watch the proportions shift. Find the shoe height that is most flattering with each hemline.

THE FOUR BASIC BODY TYPES

Now that you begin to understand the function of proportion and line in fashion and how they can make or break your look, let's get down to the specifics: you, your body, your proportions, and your best lines.

The perfectly proportioned body is composed of a harmony of parts—neck, shoulders, torso, bust, waist, hips, thighs, buttocks, and legs are all well shaped and well suited to one another. However, most of us do not have a perfectly proportioned body and at least a few of these parts deviate from the ideal. For instance, a long neck, medium-sized bust, and long waist may be accompanied by large hips and short legs. How well each of us looks in our clothes is determined by how well we learn to work with these separate figure components individually and as a whole.

In the following discussion it's important to remember one essential point about these deviations from the ideal: they are not necessarily bad. They are "variables" not "terribles." Susan Forrestal, a very successful model and a good friend of mine, has the most classic set of sloping shoulders in the business as well as one of the longest necks in town. But instead of cursing the gods that she was short-changed, she chuckles about it, praises the virtues of shoulder pads, and cheerfully relates stories about photographers who have likened her to a Modigliani.

Shelley Smith is another supermodel (you've probably seen her extolling the virtues of Lip Quencher on TV commercials and looking beautiful in the pages of *Vogue* and *Bazaar*) who is quick to admit that her proportions are far from perfect. Shelley has an extra-short waist and arms and legs like "Stella D'Oro breadsticks" (these are Shelley's words, not mine). In deference to Shelley I

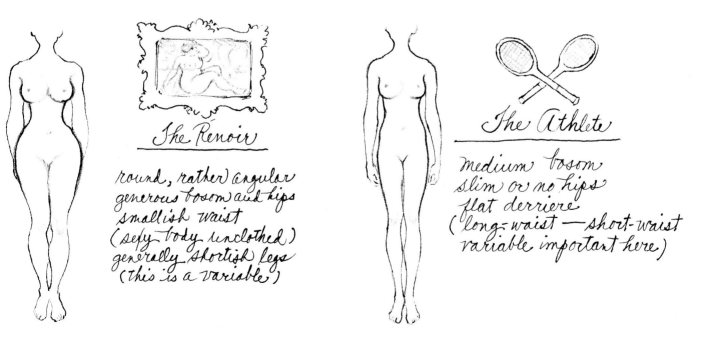

The Renoir

round, rather angular
generous bosom and hips
smallish waist
(sexy body unclothed)
generally shortish legs
(this is a variable)

The Athlete

medium bosom
slim or no hips
flat derriere
(long-waist — short-waist
variable important here)

won't continue, though I have her permission to tell all. The point is, she is not perfectly proportioned, she knows it, and she understands how to work within these limitations to produce splendid results.

And there are others: Lauren Hutton constantly jokes about her "banana nose," crossed eyes, and the space in between her two front teeth. Barbara Feldon confessed that Buck Henry once told her that her legs went up to her armpits. Anne Holbrook would prefer nice trim ankles to her own, which she jokingly likens to "chipmunk pouches." (For those of you with similar chipmunk-pouch ankles, Anne recommends a shoe with a good heel—"three inches is best"—and a skirt length that falls just below the knee without cutting into the calf.) Susan Blakeley admits that she's always felt her waist was too thick and derrière too flat, but she hit the nail right on the head when she said we all tend to be our own worst critics. The bottom line is to understand your propor-

tions, learn how to deal with them, and not be intimidated by your flaws. *Nobody is perfect.* And those you might *think* are perfect don't consider themselves so. Is it any comfort to you to know that, at least in their own eyes, they are in the same position as you and I?

On these pages are drawings of the four basic body types. They are: (1) the *Renoir* (or *Gibson Girl*) Body Type, recognizable for its lush, curvy, and voluptuous shape; (2) the *Athletic* Body Type, whose slim hips will look right at home in jodhpurs and riding boots; (3) the *Pear-Shape* Body Type, narrow on the top and full on the bottom like a ripe Bosc pear; (4) the *Easy-Chair Bulge* Body Type, a generally slender form that tends to accumulate a little extra bulk on the upper thighs and derrière. These general body types will differ according to specific variables that are listed, along with their best bets and risks, on the following chart.

Pear Shape

narrow shoulders
slim on top
smallish bosom
medium-size waist
(usually short waisted,
but this is a variable)
large hips —— most weight
concentrated here

The Easy Chair

small frame
generally slender —— more angular
small to medium bosom
average waist
average hips
thighs large for frame
variations —— long or short waist

PROPORTION VARIABLES: BEST

SMALL BODY— UNDER 5'3"

best bets
Concentrate on simplicity and long linear design
Pleated skirts (sharp vertical lines)
Slacks (long leg, fitted waist)
One color—head to toe (with different tones for interest)
Accentuate a long line from waist to feet
Long sleeves
Medium-width belts
Silk and other fabrics that move with body
Subtle vertical stripes
Smooth short-hair furs
Fitted jackets

risks
Wild, large prints
Horizontal stripes
Loose draped garments
Frills and fancy lace
Pegged-leg pants
Bulky fabrics (thick knotty wools, big furs)
Too many colors

SHORT NECK

best bets
V-necks
Open collars
Tapered hairstyles
Scoop necks

risks
Classic T-shirts
Heavy bulky scarves
Turtlenecks
High collars
Mandarin collars
Jewel-neck collars

LONG NECK

best bets
Turtlenecks
Cowl necks
Shirts worn over shirts or sweaters
Boat necks
Scarves and jewelry at neck
One-shouldered evening dresses
Hairstyles that cover nape of neck
Oxford collars

risks
Peter Pan collars
Scoop necks
Square necks
Dolman sleeves

BROAD SHOULDERS

best bets
Raglan sleeves
Drop shoulders
Dolman sleeves
Full coats
V-necks
Strapless tops

risks
Padded shoulders
Cap sleeves
Puff sleeves
Broad horizontal-stripes
Boat necks
Strapless gowns

NARROW SHOULDERS

best bets
Shirts with set-in sleeves
Padded shoulders
Dropped shoulders
Small collars
V-necks
Boat necks
Smooth short-hair furs
Halter tops

risks
Full-cut big tops
Largish coats and jackets
Turtlenecks
Bulky fabric

SLOPING SHOULDERS

best bets
Shirts with set-in sleeves
Blouses with small yokes
Padded shoulders
Spaghetti straps

risks
Raglan sleeves
Strapless tops

FULL BUST

best bets
Loose tops (not too full)
V-necks
Open collars
Silk shirts

risks
Tube top
Dolman sleeves
Tight knits
Tight blouses
Princess lines
Patch pockets on shirts or dresses
Lightweight fabrics that reveal bra lines
Clinging fabrics
Puffy sleeves

SMALL BUST

best bets
Easy, flowing blouses

risks
Tight shirts (if full-hipped)

BETS AND RISKS

LONG TORSO

best bets

High-rise slacks (straight leg, falling over shoe)
Skirts (length just below knee)
Wide belts
Vests (double layers)
Separates

risks

Low-rise pants (such as hip huggers)
Short hemlines
Belts worn low on the hips

SHORT TORSO

best bets

Slacks that ride low on natural waist)
Jacket and tunic lengths falling to inseam or just above
Sweaters worn over slacks or skirts
Overblouses

risks

Wide belts
Low-rise pants
Very short jackets
Belted tunics
Skirts with wide waistbands

THICK WAIST

best bets

Vests
Loose waistlines
Belts (worn on hips)
Tunic tops
Slacks with pleats
Blouson-style shirts and dresses
Unfitted jackets
Focus attention away from waist

risks

Nipped-in waists
Wide or wrap belts
Skirts that pleat or gather at the waist

SMALL WAIST

best bets

Nipped-in waists
Focus attention on waist with interesting belts
Belted tunics

risks

Exaggerated blouson styles
Vests, that cover sides of waist
Unbelted tunic tops
Shapeless dresses

HIGH WAIST

See short torso

LOW WAIST

See long torso

See too-long torso

AMPLE HIPS, THIGHS, BUTTOCKS

best bets

Skirts that hug top of hips and fall gently
Slacks and skirts in simple designs
Darker color bottoms or single-color outfits
Straight-line tunic tops that end at inseam
Focus attention on upper body with color, jewelry, or scarves
Substantial-weight fabrics
Loose slacks

risks

Large plaids
Broad horizontal stripes
Loud-colored bottoms
Tight slacks
Skirts with excess pleats or gathering at hips
Lightweight jersey fabrics that cling
Wide-wale corduroy
Over-the-knee boots
Very tight shirts
Dirndl skirts
Slacks with back pockets

SMALL TO NO HIPS

best bets

Skirts (pleated, dirndl)
Flapper-style loose dresses
Loose, pleated slacks
Substantial-weight fabrics
Overshirts

risks

Tight skirts
Tight, badly cut slacks
Hip huggers

SHORT LEGS

best bets

Keep waist above natural waistline
Loose trousers (long straight leg falling over shoe)
Vertical lines
Solid colors—head to toe (with accents for interest)
Long skirts (worn with boots)
Heeled shoes
Bathing suits (cut high on hips)

risks

Pegged-legged pants
Hip huggers
Low-riding belts
Bulky-texture bottoms that add dimension
Wild prints or plaids
Horizontal stripes
Thick wide-wale corduroy

HEAVY LEGS

best bets

Slacks (straight-leg cut)
Boots
Skirts (slight dirndl, worn over knee)
Shorts (wide pleats and wide bottoms)

risks

Short skirts
Extra-tight pants

Because there are so many individual variables within each type, it's impossible to give a definitive set of rules that will universally apply. So here's what to do. First, look at the sketches of the basic body types—ten to one you'll recognize your own general shape or a variation on the theme. These classic body types will help you spot what you consider are your *imperfections*. Then turn to the *Proportion Problems Variables* chart and locate your problem area. There you will find *best bets* (the lines and styles that will minimize your imperfections and be most flattering) and *risks* (the lines and styles that may emphasize your imperfections and that are therefore to be avoided).

I have labeled these rules of fashion "best bets" and "risks" rather than "do's" and "don'ts" for a very essential reason. There are always intangible factors to fashion—your personality, your mannerisms, the way you carry yourself, the way you feel. They affect the way each one of us looks in our clothes. Whether you opt for a risk item or not is your decision. I will be satisfied as long as *you know* it is a risk, and this book will tell you why it is a risk.

For you to understand why your best bets are just that—good ideas for your body type and variables—and why you should approach any risks with caution, let's examine them in more detail.

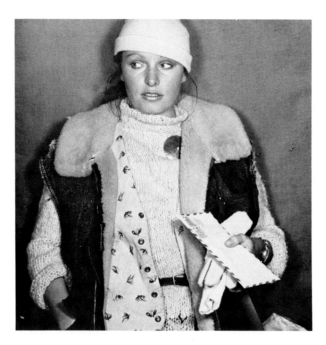

Overlayering and bulky fabrics are a risk for small women.

hanging pictures on a wall—the smaller the wall, the fewer pictures you can hang on it. If you hang too many pictures on a small wall, it will look cluttered. Likewise, if you put large prints, broad stripes, or lots of layers on your small frame, you'll look cluttered and your overall impact will be minimized. All your risks are geared to avoid this, and all your best bets are aimed toward a neat, trim, simple, linear design.

Small women (5 feet 3 inches and under)

If you are a small person, regardless of your body type, the essential thing to remember is that you have a "small fashion canvas"—you have less area to work with than a larger person. Therefore you should keep your fashion relatively uncomplicated. You can think of it as

Necks

SHORT NECKS. These can easily be elongated with certain hairstyles and collars and necklines that expose more of the chest:

1. The linear extension of the V-neck adds length to the neck, and is therefore most flattering. Any collar that abruptly cuts off the

neck from the rest of the body should be avoided. This is a common mistake. While you might think that this type of collar is showing as much neck as possible, it is not. The neck will look longer if more of the neckline is uncovered from the bottom of the chin to the cleavage.

2. A shoulder-length hairstyle that gently covers each side of the neck will give the appearance of a longer neck.

3. I don't advise turtlenecks, but if you really like them and feel they're a must for you, choose the lighter-weight variety. The less bulk at the neck the better.

LONG NECKS are beautiful and are often a definite fashion asset because of the many options they provide. The following tips will help you make the most of a long neck:

1. Cowl necks and turtlenecks look fabulous, worn separately or together. For instance, over a lightweight wool turtleneck sweater you can wear a cowl-necked sweater of another color.

Another winning look is a lightweight turtleneck covered by a man-tailored shirt. Katharine Hepburn has been wearing this style for years, and it still works. Or, a cowl-necked sweater and a big overshirt or bulky sweater can also make a smart combination.

2. Slightly oversized mandarin collars are good, but avoid little "Peter Pan"-type collars.

The deep V neckline makes a short neck appear longer (above). *A mandarin collar* (below) *is most compatible with a long neck.*

Long necks can accommodate turtle-necks and cowl necks, but these styles are much too bulky for short necks.

3. Smallish collars that can be turned up in the back work well. If you leave the shirt unbuttoned to the cleavage, it will dramatize the length of your neck. If you feel that your neck looks too bare, you can add a scarf or jewelry.

4. Boat necks seem to work better than scoop necklines or necklines that stop at the base of the neck.

5. Wearing your hair short is fine. But it's generally better to keep it longer in back so that it covers the nape of your neck.

Shoulders

Your shoulders will be either broad, narrow, sloping, or average. Shoulder width is important because it greatly influences the way a garment will hang on your frame and thus affects the drape of a particular style blouse or dress. Accommodating shoulder width is basically a matter of common sense.

BROAD SHOULDERS. Broad shoulders are likely to be more of a plus than a minus. Anne Holbrook, for instance, blesses her broad shoulders. They turn her rather smallish frame into a perfect sample dress size. Anne figures that without this asset her modeling income would be cut in half. If you want to minimize your shoulders, however, the trick is to stay away from anything that visually squares them off: look to styles that are set in from the shoulders, such as raglan or dolman sleeves. A halter top that ties around the neck is better than standard tank tops for the same reason—

Shoulders

narrow

broad

average

sloping

the tank top tends to square off the shoulders while the line of the halter makes the torso (and thus the shoulders) look narrower. A V-neck top with drop sleeves would probably be the best of all—the V would elongate the neck at the same time that the shoulders were being minimized. Broad shoulders would be made to appear average.

NARROW SHOULDERS. Narrow shoulders are rarely a problem if you're more or less narrow all over. However, if you're narrow on the top and broad on the bottom, your clothes can help equalize the discrepancy. Tops that add width are best, and the squarer the shoulder, the more width you get—boat necks are good because they create a horizontal line across the shoulders. If your top is too tight or narrow your hips will automatically look larger. Wearing a darker color on the bottom or an overall one-tone look will also help to minimize the hips. Jackets and shirts with padded shoulders are a natural. Halter tops will work, but if you are very broad on the bottom, stay away from tight ones.

The basic principles behind the advice for narrow shoulders also holds true for *sloping shoulders.* The idea is to square them off. Set-in shoulders are good, especially those with a gathering at the shoulder seam. The more substantial the fabric of a garment, the better it will hold a definite shape rather than conform to yours. Avoid any oversized bows, scarves, or jewelry. Their bulk will emphasize your small shoulders. Padded shoulders are an excellent way to add extra width. Spaghetti straps are flattering also, because they, too, visually square off the shoulders.

Best bets for women with narrow shoulders—extended-, padded-, and dropped-shoulder styles.

Bust lines

Big bust lines, while considered sexy by some, take special consideration in a contemporary fashion silhouette. If you're tall and bosomy, you'll have relatively few difficulties because your torso will be proportionately long enough to carry the extra dimension. If you're short, on the other hand, a large bosom tends to dominate the whole upper portion of your body. Any style that shortens the torso would be self-defeating, which is why wide belts and an empire line are not flattering. Any garment that is tight fitting will accentuate what is under it; if you want to minimize your bust line, you should wear relatively loose-fitting tops (perhaps gathered shoulders) of simple design. Remember, too, that a good bra is essential. Shop around until you find the right one for you. An ill-fitting bra can destroy an otherwise good fashion look.

Dressing a small-busted figure presents

Patch pocket styles will make a large bust more obvious and should be avoided by women who are generously endowed.

A blouse with an easy drape will help minimize a large bust.

relatively few problems. It's always easier to add visual dimension than to subtract it. My basic advice is to count your blessings—besides being very much in vogue these days, small breasts are best able to withstand the toll of time. If, however, you do not want your small bust to be apparent, simply stay away from tight-fitting tops. Wear soft, bloused tops with a gathering or shirring at the shoulders or a smocked front.

Patch pockets and shirring at the shoulders make a small bust less noticeable.

To best complement a full-busted figure, avoid stiff, bulky vests (above), *and opt for a gentle, draped style.*

Waistlines

Waistlines come in four varieties—small, thick, short, and long—of which the first is by far the easiest to deal with.

SMALL WAISTLINES. Having a small waist is anything but a problem; indeed, it's a boon. A naturally small waist is almost universally accepted as the ideal, so play it up. Good-looking, interestingly detailed belts should be a definite part of your wardrobe, as well as dresses that can be nipped at the waist and skirts and slacks that fit the waist snugly and accentuate it.

THICK WAISTLINES. Thick waists are common and not that much of a fashion problem. Simply don't emphasize the waist. Blouson-style dresses are a perfect foil, as are easy, shapeless dresses that can be belted below the natural waistline and slightly draped on top. The basic guideline is to wear garments that are not tight at the waist or that help mask it, such as vests, overshirts, and cardigans.

It is much more tricky to deal with the long-waist–short-waist variable. Let's look into this in more detail. Many people have trouble determining whether they are actually long waisted, short waisted, or average. There is one surefire way to spot this elusive variable without bothering with tape measures.

Once again, stand relatively unclothed in front of your full-length mirror. This time you'll need a small mirror; a compact mirror will do. Because this variable is easier to spot from behind, you will want to take a look at your entire back side, from head to toe. With your back toward the full-length mirror, look at yourself in your hand mirror. Raise your arms a little so that your silhouette is clearly in view.

If you are *short waisted*, the distance from your waist indentation to the bottom of your buttocks will look longer than the distance from your waist indentation to your armpits.

If you are *long waisted*, the opposite will be true: the distance from your waist indentation to your armpits will be longer than the distance from waist indentation to the bottom of your buttocks.

If you are *average*, these distances will be more or less evenly divided.

SHORT WAISTED. Since this is where I fit in, I know the short-waisted variable well. I'm delighted that I have long legs, but the catch is that I have very little area to work with above the waist. Ideally I would like to preserve my long-legged look, but I have to be careful not to make my torso appear any shorter than it already is. Here, then, are some very personal best bets:

1. The taller you are (i.e., the longer your

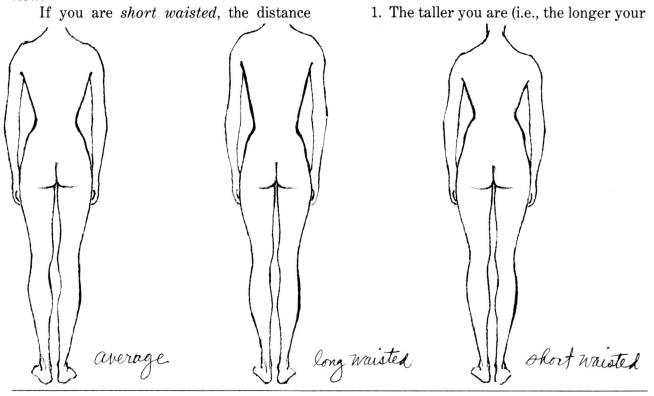

average   long waisted   short waisted

A long jacket or tunic makes the body appear shorter; a short jacket gives a longer look to the body.

a *stiff* wide belt, one you can pull relatively tight and that will not shift, you can visually lower your waistline a good inch or more. The dress will fall gracefully over the top of the belt (and your natural waistline) in a blouson style, and your new longer waist will look small because of the width and snugness of the belt. The waistline will appear to be at the bottom of the belt (an inch or more below the natural waist), and the soft, natural, linear fall of the skirt will give a long appearance to the legs. It is a nice casual look, and believe it or not, it's comfortable.

legs), the longer your tunics and jackets can fall, because you can afford to cover the leg a little more. Jackets and tunics are most flattering when they fall just a tad above where inner seams of your pants join (the inseam). If you are over 5 feet 7 inches, I would advise having your jackets and tunics end at the inseam, rather than just above it.

When considering proportion, I have found these differentials in length, although subtle, to be very important. I definitely look shorter if my jacket is too long because it interferes with my leg length, and that is what creates the illusion of my being taller than I am.

2. Wide belts are generally not good. If you wear them at your natural waistline, they end up right below the bustline, leaving very little torso in view. If you try to wear them below the natural waistline, they have a tendency to slide up. If they are too pliable, they will fold up and become narrow.

The one wide-belt exception I've noted is that if you belt a soft, easy-flowing dress with

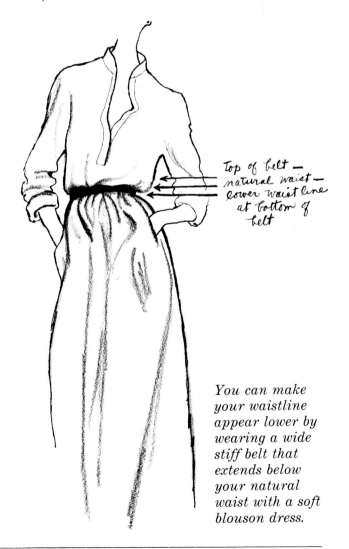

Top of belt —
natural waist —
lower waist line
at bottom of
belt

You can make your waistline appear lower by wearing a wide stiff belt that extends below your natural waist with a soft blouson dress.

Make the most of a small waist with dresses and shirts that can be nipped in at the waist (opposite page). Vests that cover the sides of the waist and tunics will help mask a thick waist.

3. Short-waisted people always seem to look better and to feel more comfortable in pants than in skirts. This is because it's very difficult to keep a skirt hanging low on the natural waistline, and when a skirt hangs on a natural waistline that is too high, the short torso is emphasized. Also, since the distance from the waist to the knee is extra long and can easily seem out of proportion to the rest of the body, skirt lengths have to be adjusted and readjusted, depending on the style and proportion of the shirts worn with them. Personally, I don't like to have to think too much when I get dressed or when I shop, so I generally stick to slacks or dresses.

Pants that hang low on the natural waist are best, because a rise that is too high will cut and emphasize the short torso (and a rise that's too low will shorten the leg). Pants are easier to proportion with tops than skirts, and dresses in a blouson style are equally easy to proportion with belts and shoes. In that case, the only added consideration is the hem length.

4. A blouse that is open to the waist will emphasize the length of the torso. I often wear

camisoles or tube tops under shirts open to the waist. This is also a good way to add another color.

LONG-WAISTED. While it is true that you can have both a long torso and long legs, this would mean that your body is evenly proportioned, putting you in (or near) the ideal category. Generally, if you have a long waist, you will have shortish legs. To make your legs appear longer:

1. Stay away from low-rise pants (hip huggers—the most extreme—are the worst style). A high-rise trouser or, for that matter, any high waist will make the legs appear longer.

2. High-heeled shoes elongate the leg. But don't go overboard: keep comfort in mind, especially during the day, if you run around a lot. Save your elegant high heels for evening wear.

3. Have the hem of your pants fall to the instep of your shoe. You want to make the line from the waist to the shoe as long as possible.

Shirts open to the waist add length to the torso by extending its vertical line.

A monochromatic outfit (left and right center) *will help give the impression of greater height because there is no color change to break the line. Notice, once again, the substantial difference that jacket lengths can make to your overall look. The longer the jacket, the shorter the legs appear.*

Wide belts can make the waist appear higher (left).

For a time the trend was to wear slim pants tied at the ankle—or very pegged-leg pants—a great look on very long legs. Neither is flattering to short legs. You can still keep the silhouette neat and trim without an exaggerated pegged leg. A narrow straight-lined pant leg will give you the look you want without diminishing the leg length. This is a good example of modifying a trend to work for your body type.

4. A single color will create a longer-legged look. The eye won't initially discern where the leg begins. The color and silhouette will be the main focal point. A line can easily be broken by a change of color.

5. Wide belts will make the waist appear higher, and any belt placed above the natural waistline will visually raise the waist and thus lengthen the leg.

There are some advantages to being long waisted. (As a matter of fact, if they were accepting orders for new bodies, I would put in for an extra inch or two in my torso.) The more space above the belt, the more fashion options in that area.

▫ You can layer two shirts, vests, a dress and shirt, wear a few scarves, and so on.

This kind of layered look is a natural for long-waisted women.

34

□ Almost any fashion will work if you remember to keep the leg looking long. Skirts and dresses properly proportioned to your body type are ideal and easy to wear.

Buttocks, hips, and thighs

If you are one of the lucky ones with relatively slim hips, thighs, and buttocks, you're on your own; you really don't need much guidance. But a warning—watch out for baggy, polyester pants. They won't help you make the most of your slender silhouette.

If you are somewhat heavy in these areas, at least know that you have a lot of company. Hips, thighs, and derrières are common trouble spots for women. "In women there is a tendency to the massing of fat on the outer side of the thigh, just below the level of the trochanter (a muscle on the outer thigh)." (*A Handbook of Anatomy for Art Students*, Arthur Thompson, Dover.) This alarming statement is from one of my college art anatomy books. I didn't like hearing about the tendency to amass fat then—and I like it even less now. However, it is a fact, and we have to deal with it. Even I, whom most people think of as on the skinny side, have to exercise daily to keep from adding an unsightly dimension to my upper thighs.

There are ways of dressing to help visually eliminate this bulge until you can really get rid of it (I would feel I'd slighted you if I didn't strongly recommend that you begin a regular program of exercise.) This proportion variable is one that I know well, and I also know how substantially it reduces one's style

Skirts with gentle pleats or gathers at the front and back will help disguise generous hips and thighs. Tight straight skirts are a definite risk.

Tunics of this length look best on tall women. They would be too long for short and even average women and would tend to make them look smaller.

options. While a firm roundness may be rather pleasant, unsightly bulges only get in the way.

Until diet, exercise, and discipline show results, here are a few safe bets:

1. Tunic tops are good. But watch the length. If you wear them too long, they will make your legs appear shorter. It's not always necessary to cover the problem area completely. If you're relatively thin, except for the outer-thigh area, keep the line from the shoulders to mid-thigh straight. The bulge will hardly be noticeable.

2. Never wear tight pants. Nothing makes bulges more obvious, except maybe Saran wrap. Loose, easy slacks worn with a fairly loose-fitting blouse that is tucked in and belted

I dress for my personality and for what's right for me. I try not to dress just because of fashion.
MAUD ADAMS

You must take a good look at yourself and understand what you can wear. Find out the good things that you want to emphasize, then really emphasize them.
POLLY MELLEN

Tight pants are the wrong choice for full-hipped women, but pants need not be completely ruled out. Straight-legged slacks in a full cut can work quite well.

will create a stylish look, without drawing attention to problem areas. Dresses and skirts are always good.

3. Darkish colors are better than bright, startling ones. An overall dark look, with a focal point near the face—an interesting piece of jewelry, a striking scarf—will lead an admiring eye away from your hips and thighs to your face, where your sparkling personality can take over.

4. The basic rule of thumb here is to keep things simple in the problem area. Less is more. Get tricky or flashy elsewhere.

I hope that I have shown you that no matter what your body type there are still many clothing styles that will be flattering to you and will help you look your best. Part of the excitement and challenge of fashion is in learning to work with what you have and to create the illusion of perfection.

Now that we've looked at the basics of dressing your body type, it's time to have some fun with the creative possibilities of color and texture and add zest with accessories.

When you supply your body with all the nutrition it needs, you'll look good, your body will stay in shape, you'll be nice and trim, and you'll feel great—have a lot of energy and vitality. Then when you put clothes on top of all this health, you're a winner.
BEVERLY JOHNSON

COLOR SCHEMES

SOLIDS, PATTERNS, AND COLOR PLAY

While proportion is the most subtle fashion factor, I think color is the one that is the most fun. By using color effectively, you can create a mood or feeling. You can choose to be a breath of spring in mixed pastels, or a ray of summer sunshine in whites and pale yellows. You can be sexy and demure in black or racy and dynamic in bright red.

Every day you are confronted with innumerable colors, shades, and tones, and the only limitations on how you use them are your flexibility, your imagination, and your coloring (hair color and skin tone). Let's talk about flexibility first.

In order to be flexible in your approach to anything, you have to keep an open mind and rid yourself of old taboos. Fashion is no exception. Forget all the poppycock you've heard through the years about which colors "go" and which colors are "right" for summer, winter, spring, or fall. Colors are seasonless. What could be more refreshing on a gloomy winter day than a lovely pastel sweater?

But, you may answer, the seasons themselves produce the colors we associate with them. So what? Who says we have to blend into the background? Happily, we can now make our own color decisions. Contrast can provide an effective alternative to conformity, much as asymmetry offers relief from symmetry. Stephen Burrows, one of today's most innovative designers, uses asymmetrics as one of his basic design techniques. To quote Stephen: "I don't like designs to be the same on each side; I like things to look a little lopsided.... I prefer everything to be unmatched—lines, textures, and colors. The key words are flexibility and individualism." Environment does of course play an important role in your choices.

Obviously, if you are in an executive position with a conservative old-line company, you're not going to opt for a bright yellow dress with a purple scarf flung nonchalantly about your neck to wear to a meeting with the president. It simply wouldn't make sense. You not only would stick out like a Day-glo decal against wood paneling, you would be presenting an image that might be harmful to your professional life.

Selecting fashion colors requires an understanding of your surroundings on vacations and business trips as well. Because the quality of light and general atmosphere vary from place to place, travel wardrobes may require some special color planning. In New York, for example, I almost always feel comfortable in black—but it was the wrong choice for my recent vacation to Greece. Every old woman I passed was wearing it. I quickly decided that black seemed too somber for the carefree, easy environment. These distinctions can be equally true on the same continent, where the feeling can differ from coast to coast. What works in New York may not work in L.A. Erin Grey understands this better than most since she divides her time between the two: "I adore white in L.A. I don't wear any of my black clothes there. But when I come to New York I always bring my black clothes with me. I know I'm going to want to put them on. Even my makeup—the amount and the color of the foundation—changes in New York. The lighting is different. If I wear the same heavy makeup that I wear in New York in L.A., I feel like a clown. It's simply too harsh for California."

Color evokes a mood and creates a strong initial impression. This outfit owes more to the dynamic quality of red than to its essentially simple design.

White is seasonless. Whether in winter wools or summer linens, it has a pure, refreshing quality.

Personality and mood are equally important factors in our reaction to the colors we wear. Listen to my friend Betsy's "red story":

A year or two ago I went to Clovis Ruffin to buy a dress for a wedding. I tried on a terrific red dress. When I asked if they had it in another color, everybody in the room told me how great it looked, that red did wonders for me; I had to have it. Anyway, they talked me into it. I wore it to the wedding and felt really uncomfortable. I know I looked good—blond hair and bright red is a great combination—and even my husband complimented me. But it didn't matter. I felt uncomfortable. I felt that I showed too much. Let's face it, there's no way to hide or fade into the background in a fire-engine-red dress.

So it is apparent how very individual one's choice of color is. Perry Ellis, another of today's most popular designers, works primarily with muted colors and is very conscious of the influence of personality on color choice.

It's the subtlety of colors that I really love . . . the interplay of grays and tans and all those sorts of colors, combined.

I really like color on many people; I'm just not extroverted enough to deal in it. But there are no rights and wrongs with color. I have an actress friend with black hair and white skin, and when she wears turquoise or red, she looks spectacular. For her to dress in gray is to go unnoticed. She's not meant for that; she needs color. Because I don't use color doesn't make it right; it is merely what I like, my personal statement. Other designers do color, and it's terrific for them and their customers. We are all very different, and we have to know ourselves to know what we really want and need. That doesn't mean you only have to be one way. Today it can be neutrals, and tomorrow it can be color—it's how you're feeling. Absolutely anything is possible.

Willi Smith, whose creative designs are very different from Perry's, also clearly understands the individuality of color selection. "What I usually do," he says, "is design everything in a range of five to seven colors. What I like to do is break those down into three color groups, the tones of which can be mixed, from warms to cools. There are people who generally wear only blues and grays; those who like the brights—red, orange, yellow; and those who favor the neutrals—who live only in beige."

Today's clothing and accessories offer us an endless array of colors to choose from. The combinations you can put together are vast.

SOLIDS

A good safe way to begin playing with color is to start with *solids*. Forget patterns, plaids, and stripes for the time being. Dressing in solid colors is simple, effective, and, I might add, economical. You can mix different solid-colored shirts, dresses, and camisole-type under tops or scarves, tunics, slacks, skirts, and belts almost without thinking.

Combinations of clear, intense colors provide a special interest to basically simple designs.

I dress in solid colors more often than not. I know, for example, that I look good in white, black, bright red, bright blue, and turquoise. These colors pretty much dominate my wardrobe in one way or another. They all complement one another, and me. I can wear white pants, a bright blue shirt, and a white overshirt belted in a tunic style; then I roll up the sleeves on the white shirt so the blue cuffs show, and presto—I look great! The white serves as a contrast to my dark skin and hair and the electric blue around my face gives me an extra spark.

Once you have the hang of one color scheme, it's simple to master another. For instance, I can apply the same principles of my "white look" to a primarily black outfit, using a red shirt for the spark. Here, instead of contrasting my black hair and dark skin with white, I am complementing them with a like color, black. I can also mix white with red, black and white with a touch of red, red and turquoise, or turquoise and black. I can go all white or all black or all turquoise and just add one accessory for an extra zap, possibly a fabulous purple belt.

I'm not the only one who has limited her color palette. A lot of the women I have talked with deal with color in a similar manner. Pam Suthern, who has blue eyes and sandy-colored hair, works her wardrobe applying this solid-color principle and using *her* colors—navy, beiges, and mauves. Margrit Ramme, a very light-blonde model, works her wardrobe around the earth tones and muted shades—putty, beiges, browns, grays. "Everything just goes together. I hardly have to think about color when I get dressed in the morning." And Maud Adams favors tans and whites: "I buy things that all mix and match. I have a basic wardrobe that works with everything. This

A dash of bright color at the wrist and a bright shirt is all you need for accent with a neutral jacket and skirt.

matter of basic composition. A good painting has good composition, and so does good fashion; in both cases, there are many approaches that will work equally well. Bill Blass and Stephen Burrows, for instance, have a very different sense of composition, yet each creates wonderful designs.

You'll find that you can mix almost any primary or opposite colors with no problems. The primary colors are red, blue, and yellow. Their opposite colors are those directly facing them on the simple color chart on this page. Almost any color will perk up white or black.

year I bought mostly beiges, browns, and off-whites—all tan colors, light for the summer. This might sound boring, but it's not when you realize you can add almost anything to pep it up—like a red blouse, for instance."

Nearly everything can be simplified and made to work well. Many variations can be created without overloading your wardrobe, and all the variations will be incredibly effective and make a total statement. And as a dividend, color coordination makes organizing a travel wardrobe a cinch.

The key thing to keep in mind with this kind of dressing is color balance. It is not merely matching colors, but creating a total balance of colors and harmony of tones within your fashion scheme. This is easy to understand if you think of dressing as painting a picture. Your body is the canvas. The paints are the colors (and textures) of your clothes. Hence putting clothes on your body becomes a

Almost all colors go together. Here, the American classic—red, white, and blue—and a range of muted dark pastels in complementary hues.

The drawings on this page are illustrations of various color compositions. In the first series, we have taken a pair of off-white slacks and a matching shirt that can be worn in or out (this is about as close to a blank canvas as you can get). The addition of colors—tan and red—creates a different look. This kind of composition is easy—it's like dabbing red and tan paint on a white canvas. Almost any combination of these colors you can come up with will work. Even bringing in another color, such as blue (figure 5), will work, as long as it is not a dark tone. Any dark color would stand out like a sore thumb without other dark colors to help balance it. Light colors are recessive and therefore do not create much of a problem of balance; dark colors are dominant and require special attention when being introduced. See what happens when I add black shoes (figure 6). They appear too heavy in comparison to the other colors in the outfit.

In the second series of sketches, we have taken a dark gray skirt and light beige blouse and balanced the light and dark with two mid-tone colors—red and medium gray. With the light color on top, the balance is fairly easy to achieve. When we reverse the colors of the skirt and blouse, putting the light color on the bottom, you can see that balance becomes more of a problem. The dark shoes in these drawings play an important role in keeping the outfit from looking top heavy. A light color on the upper half of the body can easily be broken up and tied in with the rest of the outfit with jewelry, scarves, and third layers (such as jacket, sweater, and vest) in darker or contrasting colors. These clothing and accessory options are not available to break up a light color on the lower half of the body and to create a balance of colors in the outfit. This is one of the reasons most of us have been taught it is wrong to wear lighter colors on the bottom of an outfit. It is not wrong—it will just be more difficult to achieve balance. Because light colors tend to make us appear larger and dark colors tend to minimize our breadth, a woman

1   2   3   4   5   6

with very large hips would do best to keep her darker colors on the bottom half of her body (see figures 7–9).

Pastel shades and their muted variations are no more difficult to deal with than the primaries. They can all be mixed; which ones you wear together is just a matter of personal preference. For instance, you could try pairing lavender and pale blue or pale yellow, beige and pale pink, salmon and pale blue. As long as you stay more or less within the same intensity, anything will work. Generally, one color should predominate.

Although the darker fashion shades—including navy, burgundy, forest green, and brown—can mix, they are often more effective when combined with a slightly lighter or more brilliant color. For instance, navy can be perked up with red, white, or emerald green; brown and forest green work well with tan; and burgundy looks great with rose, light blue, or any of the new muted tones of gray, green, and beige.

If you keep your eyes open, you'll see lots of color combinations you might not have considered pass right before your eyes. When I was driving down a country road one day at dusk, a tan Mercedes passed me with its red taillights ablaze. The red and tan combination caught my eye—I thought it was sensational—so I added a pair of tan slacks and a couple of natural leather belts to my wardrobe.

Unexpected color combinations can also come right out of your wardrobe. Next time you decide to explore the inner recesses of your closet to reclaim clothing that is presently wearable or can be recycled, or to weed out things to send to relatives or charitable organizations, you might as well do some color experimenting while you're at it.

As you sort through your belongings, put aside every piece of clothing you spot in a new and different color or tone, including scarves, old jackets or sweaters, and even linings of skirts and coats. Separate the prints and patterns from the solid colors.

7   8   9   10   11   12

49

Pastel colors lend themselves to soft and pleasing combinations. These blue and rose tones of the same value are an especially well-suited match.

When you have assembled a fairly good range of colors, look at them as if you were selecting swatches to make up a unique patchwork quilt. Using your bed or floor as a work surface, play with fabrics, pair up different primary and opposite colors, different values and tones. Try finding interesting combinations that you never before imagined would work. I guarantee that you will come up with more exciting groupings of color for your imaginary quilt than if you were consciously trying to create color combinations for your wardrobe. After you have concentrated on colors for a while, you can begin to bring in some patterns. Start experimenting with prints and colors, and then try combining prints with other prints.

The majority of these new combinations *will* work for fashion. And even the colors that you feel are not flattering to your skin tone can be part of this more varied range as long as there is a becoming color near your face.

PATTERNS

Once you have settled on your best colors, introducing stripes, plaids, and other patterns into a basic solid-colored wardrobe is a relatively easy task. The biggest problem is finding good-looking, flattering patterns. If budget is a consideration, select items that can easily be mixed and matched with the rest of your wardrobe—the more subtle the pattern, the more wear you'll get out of it.

An unexpected blend of colors creates a strong effect.

The following are a few ideas that will serve as a springboard for ways to introduce patterns into your wardrobe.

BLOUSES AND VESTS. Try wearing a red pin-striped blouse with a beige shirtwaist dress. Wear the blouse over the dress and tie it at the waist, or wear it under the shirtwaist with its collar and cuffs showing. Add a red leather belt for accent. This blouse can be paired up in the same manner with shirtwaist dresses in a variety of colors, including muted olive green, navy, gray, brown, and black. For a chic, tailored look, combine a subtly patterned vest in gray, blue, and brown tones with a simple light blue blouse and gray flannel skirt (a scarf in a very subtle print would add an extra interesting touch).

SCARVES AND BELTS. A wide, multicolored striped belt can be used to tie in a skirt and blouse in different colors. Scarves and belts can help to create a balance between stark combinations of light and dark tones. For example, a red belt would add a good, solid, mid-tone color to a navy skirt and white blouse, and a scarf in a red, white, and blue print would polish the look.

Plaid jackets or overshirts, striped tube tops or camisoles, and skirts in small prints will also help you introduce patterns into your wardrobe and will bring some interesting, useful accents to your fashion.

Mixing and coordinating patterns—prints with stripes, plaids with stripes, stripes with stripes—is somewhat difficult at first. The subtleties are very sophisticated. An excellent way to educate your eye to do this is to practice

Dressing in a modern way has to do with shape, simplicity, pure design and pure line. It involves very good fabrics, interesting mixes of fabrics and colors, and unexpected, surprising combinations.
CALVIN KLEIN

with textures first. Because the texture of a fabric can itself produce a kind of pattern, if you put a ribbed wool sweater with a nubby-tweed jacket you are in effect mixing patterns. As almost any of these texture combinations you put together will work, any mistakes you may make while in training will be minimal. Also, keep your eye on the snappier dressers among our brethren. Some men put together print ties and striped shirts in very interesting ways. If you see a combination that strikes your fancy, feel free to adapt the principle to your style.

If you are not reed thin, you would do best to stay away from wild patterns and horizontal stripes. They will make you appear larger. Nina Blanchard learned this the hard way:

I'm most comfortable in black. I have more black sweaters, black coats, black dresses, than you could imagine. One time Eileen [Ford, one of her good friends] said to me, "get out of black, wear some color for God's sake!" Well, I tried it, and I got into some prints. And I must tell you, I saw myself on a TV interview show in a beautiful Anne Klein print, and I looked like a circus elephant—it added ten pounds. I will never wear a print again unless it's the tiniest one in the world, because prints just aren't good on me. And I love them. I love paisleys. But if you're short and you want to look heavier, wear a print. It's that simple.

Plaids, prints, and stripes can be successfully combined by choosing subtle patterns within the same color family. These inspiring examples are by Calvin Klein (left) and Yves Saint Laurent (right).

The most important factor in mixing patterns well is harmony. They must not *compete* with one another. The mixture must be harmonious. One pattern should dominate over the rest. What you don't want are prints screaming at stripes, or stripes stomping on plaids. Stay in the same color family.

Be aware of the combinations you see in fashion magazines, and take a minute to figure out why they work. Watch the way the designers do it; they've been practicing for years. Calvin Klein and Yves Saint Laurent are geniuses at mixing patterns, so take a look at some of their inventive combinations. These kinds of mixtures can spur your imagination. Awareness is key.

SKIN TONE

Although I understand skin tones well, and deal with them in my work, I don't consider myself a cosmetic expert. So I called on my good friend Way Bandy, whom I have worked with for many years, to lend a hand with this section. Way's expertise in the cosmetic field is well known. His book, *Designing Your Face,*

Movement is very important to me. I hate clothes that just walk around with the woman inside them.
CYD CHARISSE

If you use a touch of white around your face, clothing in colors that are not flattering to your skin tone can be made to work.

has been a well-deserved best seller. Besides making up almost every top model in the business, Way has served as a beauty consultant to such notables as Diane Von Furstenburg, Gloria Vanderbilt, Lee Radziwill, Beverly Sassoon, and Claire Bloom (to name just a few). In short, he is tops. Here are Way's views on color and skin tones:

> Everyone is individual and has a slightly different tone of skin, but we all follow a certain range or category of skin coloration. I refer to it as light, medium, and dark. That's basically what it is. Just as someone knows that her skin is oily or dry, she knows that her skin is light, medium, or dark in color. Then too we all have various subtle colors in our skin, but basically we have either a pink or a yellow undertone (red and yellow is the way I classify it—red including all the tones of pink). If you look at the inside of your lower forearm, you can see what your undertone is. It's a good idea, though, to compare your coloration with that of others. You might look at the inside of your forearm and think it yellow, then hold it next to someone who is truly yellow and realize that you have more of a pinkish cast. Comparison is sometimes the best way to truly analyze personal skin coloring.
>
> The best way to select the proper foundation—and I think a liquid foundation, an emulsion-type that is a combination of oil and water, is best for all skin tones—is to match the foundation to the color of your neck, not to the inside of the wrist or the back of the hand, which is common practice in department stores. You're going to be putting liquid foundation or foundation base on your face and blending it slightly down the neck. Since you

don't want a line of demarcation from the face to where you blended it on the neck, matching the foundation to the skin on the side or front of the neck is your best bet. If there's no noticeable difference between neck and foundation color, you have the right foundation color for you, and you'll look as though you have no makeup on.

According to Way, it is not easy to alter your skin tone with cosmetics:

We all have a basic color aura, and I don't generally advise changing it. It gets too complicated and contrived. You would have to match the color all over—you would have to apply more makeup to your neck, which would get on your clothes, and you would even have to change the color of your hands. Unless you want to make it a lifetime job, it's hardly worth it.

Hair colors are usually related to specific undertones: redheads often have more pinkish-red undertones; brunettes more olive and yellow undertones—although there is the Irish-type brunette with very pale skin and black hair; true blonds have more pink undertones. In general, the lighter colors have a pink undertone and the darker colors a more yellow, or olive, undertone. Remember, it's the undertones that are important.

I feel very strongly that each individual has certain colors that seem to up their personal kilowatts of vibrancy and attractiveness, and it's usually within a narrow range of colors. They not only make the person look better, but feel better as well. I think that self-examination leads to a simplification of color selection—say two, three, or four colors that look best, feel best, and elicit the desired response from others. We all make a personal presentation of our inner beings by what we wear on the outside. Color is a good part of this presentation.

There are certain colors that are unflattering because of personal color auras. These colors neutralize you and work against you rather than for you. If you have a yellow undertone, for instance, mustard yellow would be an unflattering color. Pinkish undertones tend to be more flexible. Green is a color that's unflattering to most skin tones. It seems to bring out the greenness and sallowness in skins. Red, a clear China lacquer red, on the other hand, seems to look good on almost anyone, from the palest icy blonde à la Grace Kelly to someone with the very blackest skin coloration—an Ethiopian looks wonderful in a hot strong red. But it's difficult to set any definite rules for matching skin tones and colors. Perhaps one should start out with neutrals, then add accents of color that they particularly like. If they feel good with their choice of color accents, they should then gravitate in that direction. From there they can branch out into other colors they are particularly drawn to, until they settle on the colors that best express them.

Now you can see why understanding your skin tone and its undertones will make it easier for you to find *your* color, colors that enhance *you*. Consider your eye color. If your eyes are blue, wear a blue that will make them appear even bluer, and so on. And, if a color is a big seller one season and it doesn't suit you, don't feel you have to try it just because it's new.

Remember, too, that colors are made up of varying values and intensities: red, for instance, can be a bright fire-engine red, an orange red, a bluish burgundy red, and a host of other tones. When you are shopping one day, go to a mirror and hold several different

Any color that's good to the skin is good for you. That's the only thing to go by—what clears the skin and makes you feel warm toward yourself.
DIANA VREELAND

Like these reds, colors come in a variety of hues and tones. Although the variations are sometimes subtle, with a little practice you'll easily spot the tones that are best for you.

shades of your favorite colors close to your face. Try and be very objective, as if you were looking at a complete stranger, and pick the one that livens up your complexion the most. The more you look at colors, the more you will actually see them, and the better you will get to know which ones are best for you.

I have dark hair and a very olive complexion. And although I dearly love khaki, army drab green, and purples, they do nothing for me. On the contrary, they sap the glow from my skin and make me look somewhat dreary, especially in the winter, when I'm without a tan. While I generally stay away from these colors, I might, for instance, wear a pair of khaki pants, but I won't put the color near my face.

After talking with all my friends in the business; with varying skin tones and hair colors, one definite conclusion evolved—color is very individual.

COLOR: CONSUMER RATINGS

BLONDES. Over 50 percent of the blondes I talked to seemed to favor earth tones and the more muted shades—beiges, grayish greens, grayish blues. Even though bright colors are often flattering, they feel that too much color is overwhelming, and that it can dominate rather than complement their personalities.

Perhaps that's why red is a fantasy color for so many blondes. They love the color but feel uncomfortable wearing it. Pastel pink is also not a favorite of my blonde friends. Some feel there is a stigma of youth or little girlishness attached to it—and for many it conjures up images of the 1950s, of Jayne Mansfield and Mamie Van Doren and pink bathtubs, pink poodles, pink bedrooms, and pink Cadillacs.

Besides the muted tones, favored colors were black, white, navy, and deep purple.

REDHEADS. Most redheads polled concurred that they've been told since childhood that green was their color and that other colors were very chancey. While agreeing that green is sometimes a flattering color because it tends to minimize the redness in their skin, they hastened to add that hue and intensity make the difference. For this reason, sea foam, forest green, and misty gray tones were preferred. Old color taboos have pretty much been shrugged off. To quote one illustrious redhead, "Redheads should never be timid with color." Now they even wear red, a color that was high on their forbidden list, although they usually favor reds with a touch of blue in them, such as burgundies and maroons. Bubble-gum pink was unanimously rejected. Other favorites were blues, browns, camel, certain shades of purple, and magenta (fuchsia).

BRUNETTES. Brunettes polled tended to favor colors that are lively and playful. Red, bright blue, and turquoise came out on top, and white and black were also highly praised. The fact of the matter is that dark hair prevents these strong colors from becoming overpowering.

Most of the brunettes were not actually against the muted tones, but to put it in Bev Silver's words, "They really don't do anything one way or the other for me, and why wear a color that doesn't work for you? There are plenty of other colors out there ready to pitch in and help."

Pink again was in disfavor for its coy youthfulness. (Could it be a rebellion against our baby wardrobes?)

BLACK WOMEN. Although all the black women interviewed loved bright, very strong, pure colors—cobalt blue, red, emerald green, and clear strong yellow—none of them seemed to avoid any colors in particular. Beverly Johnson, one of the top black models in America today, who, while "into red" (she wears it almost every day), has gone through periods when she has worn white, beige, black, and brown more or less exclusively. And Bethann Hardison, one of the most successful runway models in the business (I can't think of one well-known designer whose collections she hasn't modeled), says she basically likes all colors because she can wear them easily and feels every one of them looks good. To put it in her words, "How could any color not look good on chocolate brown?"

Whatever their hair color or skin color, everybody liked red. Even those who did not feel comfortable wearing red themselves admired it and enjoyed seeing it on other people. It was considered dynamic, uplifting to the spirit, and flattering to most skin tones.

Black and white were close runners-up. White was praised for its fresh, clean, cool look, and again, most people thought it a flattering color for most skin tones. Black, though

All colors go —it's just a matter of how you put them together. Colors should be happy—like toys.
STEPHEN BURROWS

COLOR SCHEMES

You don't even have to be fashionable to have style. It's just a marvelous thing that people have and it's something all of their own. And it has very little to do with their clothes. The clothes just work very well for them. Fred Astaire—that's style.
DIANA VREELAND

very popular, met with some controversy; while some people considered it the most elegant color, others felt it drained their energy. Ara Gallant had one of the more interesting views:

> I think of black as inconspicuous, as no color, as something that disappears into nothing. However, if the black one wears happens to be black leather or something similar, it can become an important aspect of one's clothing, no longer just a silhouette. I wear black a lot and like it to be just a silhouette, a shape, and to have the absence of detail. I like a silhouette on me rather than a style.

There's no doubt that color is the most individual fashion choice we have.

Diana Vreeland at home, in a room of daring reds.

59

THE TOUCH FACTOR

KNOWING THE TEXTURE AND VARIETY OF FABRIC

Texture offers another exciting fashion playground. Not only can the texture of a fabric give added dimension and interest to a total look, but it can also greatly influence the way you feel. Silk, for instance, is a very sensual fabric—it feels wonderful next to your skin. I don't think there is any doubt about the fact that silk will make you feel softer and more feminine than, for example, wool or leather. The feel, or texture, of a fabric can affect your mood as surely as color.

The texture of a fabric is determined not only by its fiber content, but also by the type of yarn used, the weave of the yarn, and the fabric finish. Thus one fiber can produce a huge variety of textures. Think of the amazing multitude of textures that a fiber such as cotton can produce: corduroy, denim, muslin, velveteen, velour, flannel, oxford cloth, chambray, poplin, batiste. While they are all cotton, they each feel and look incredibly different.

In fashion, all textures can be mixed; there are no rules. You can mix a rough texture such as corduroy with as soft a texture as silk—the contrast is enough to make a statement in and of itself. The essential thing in dealing with texture is to be very conscious of it, until your awareness of it becomes second nature. How many times have you seen a pipe-smoking "English professor" (if not on campus, on the movie screen) wearing a tweed jacket with suede elbow patches? Did you consider that it was the contrast of the smooth suede and the rough tweed that helped make the look interesting? If you didn't think of it, you are not alone. Texture is a subconscious consideration for most of us, and that is probably why we don't utilize it as well as possible in our wardrobes.

Texture helps define the character of an outfit. While all these clothes are made from cotton, they look and feel incredibly different.

The many possibilities for contrast in a single-color outfit, combining shiny and matte textures in metallic, leather, and wool fabrics.

The softness of a satin shirt against the rough texture of denim jeans, an interesting contrast of luxury and utility fabrics.

Polly Mellen, the fashion editor at *Vogue* (and one of the most creative and savvy editors in the business), speaks of "the multiple use you can get from classic shapes with the interplay of fabrics and textures." She concurs with Bill Blass and Calvin Klein that it is the unexpected element of contrast that can add individuality to your look: you can bring whimsy or freshness to a classic tailored look or add elegance and class to a very casual look. "Always add a little surprise," as Polly puts it.

Some possible combinations for fall, spring, and winter:

☐ Flannel trousers with a linen jacket.

☐ Crew-neck sweater worn over a satin shirt, and corduroy pants. (The surprise—the satin shirt.)

☐ Well-cut jeans with boots and a silk shirt. (The silk shirt will add elegance.)

☐ Suede camisole with a silk shirt.

There can be the same interplay with summer fabrics:

☐ Cotton gauze with cotton lisle and satin.

☐ Matte jersey with linen or gauze.

☐ Chiffon shirt over a matte-jersey camisole, and a crepe de Chine skirt.

☐ Add some iridescence to a rainy day with a sweater, tights, and socks.

Texture can also help you determine the quality of a fabric. Poor-quality cloth simply feels like poor-quality cloth. Use your sense of touch as an antenna; if a fabric feels good, it's in the running. If it doesn't, rule it out. Just as you have to train your eye for color, so you must train your sense of touch for texture. Before you are truly able to judge a fabric, however, you will need some basic information about cloth. In order to acquaint you with some of the common terminologies and the general quali-

Texture, like color, helps create a mood. There's no doubt that leather is tougher than chiffon.

ties of the various fibers, I have offered a brief review of some of the important points about cloth.

It is the type of yarn or the weave of fibers that gives most cloths their generic names, not the fibers themselves. Crepe, for instance, can be made from cotton, silk, wool, rayon, or nylon. Organdy can be produced from silk, cotton, rayon, or nylon. Gabardine can be composed of cotton, wool, or rayon. The fiber is only partially responsible for a fabric's wear and feel. The basic yarn construction, weave, and fabric finish are also important determinants. And it is all of these factors combined that determines the price and look of a fabric.

The whole process starts with yarn. A yarn consists of strands of fibers or filaments, either natural or man-made, which have been grouped together or twisted for use in weaving, knitting, and other fabric constructions. The method in which this is done creates yarns of different weights, fineness, sheerness, smoothness, or nubbiness, and has a direct effect on the qualities of a fabric—its warmth, durability, weight, luster, texture. Thus before a fabric is even constructed, certain of its properties are predetermined by the choice of the type of yarn.

The next step is turning the chosen yarn into cloth. There are several methods by which this is done; the most commonly used is weaving.

Weaving is the process of interlacing two sets of yarn at right angles. You may be familiar with the process without even being aware of it. If you've ever seen somebody making straw hats on the beach during a Caribbean holiday, you've seen weaving in its most primitive form. The principle is the same for fabric weaving, only the yarns are considerably smaller than palm fronds. There are three basic fabric weaves: plain, twill, and satin.

THE PLAIN WEAVE. As its name suggests, the plain weave is the simplest. Basically the horizontal yarn is continually passed over and under the vertical yarn, interlacing the two. The result is a simple, flat, easy-to-launder cloth. The closer the weave, the more durable. Because of the simplicity of the design these fabrics are comparatively inexpensive.

Some of the common plain-weave fabrics are:

Cotton: gingham, percale, voile, crepe, batiste, calico, seersucker, chambray, cheesecloth, lawn, organdy, shantung, muslin, canvas

Silk: taffeta, organza, voile, crepe de Chine, georgette, pongee, shantung, china silk, broadcloth

Wool: batiste, challis, crepe, georgette, some tweeds, homespun, poplin, faille, flannel

Nylon: organdy, taffeta, shantung

Linens: a number of different cloths fall in this family, but their specific names are seldom used

There are a few variations of the plain weave that add interest to the fabric and produce different effects. When uneven yarns are used at irregular intervals, for instance, a roughened, bumpy texture results, such as a pongee or shantung. A ribbed effect is created when the horizontal yarns are heavier than the vertical,

On top, an attractive plain weave cotton. At the bottom, a blend of soft and rough textures, ideal for winter wear. At right, Shelley Smith in a sensual satin that flows with the movement of the body.

I love fabrics that move with the body. When I wear Ultra Suede, I feel like I should be a sofa.
SHELLEY SMITH

as is the case with poplin. And another effect is created when the two yarns are of different colors. Chambray, gingham, and madras are good examples of this variation.

THE TWILL WEAVE. This is the most durable weave. The yarns are interlaced in such a way as to form diagonal ridges across the fabric that are called wales. If the wales run in two directions instead of one, the weave is called herringbone. Fabrics made with the twill weave are closer in texture, heavier, and stronger than plain weaves, and because the process is more complicated, they cost more. Twills don't show dirt easily, but due to the ridges, once soiled they are hard to clean. This weave is used most frequently for cottons and wools. The more common twill fabrics are:

Cotton: denim, gabardine, serge, Canton flannel, ticking

Wool: flannel, tweed, broadcloth, gabardine, whipcord

THE SATIN AND SATEEN WEAVES. In a satin weave more vertical than horizontal weave is exposed. In a sateen weave the opposite is true. (It is far more complicated than this, but this will give you the essential idea.) Both these weaves produce smooth, lustrous, rich-looking fabrics, ideal for glamorous evening clothes. These weaves require more complicated machinery and thus are relatively expensive. Satins and sateen can be made in silk, cotton, rayon, and nylon.

THE OTHER WEAVES. The other weaves are commonly referred to as fancy weaves. They include pile, jacquard, dobby, and leno.

The pile weave produces fabrics with a soft, downy, texture. The right side of the fabric consists of soft, clipped yarns called pile. The wrong side of the fabric is smooth. Some pile weave fabrics are:

Cotton: velveteen, velour, terry cloth, corduroy, chenille.

Silk: velvet, velour, chenille

Wool: corduroy

Blends(synthetic and natural): velvet, velour, chenille

While all pile fabrics are warm, fabrics that are made of silk are the warmest and most beautiful. A silk velvet takes a deep, rich color, drapes better, and is less stiff than cotton velvets or other velvet fabrics. Velvet blends tend to be less expensive than velvet made from pure silk, but may lack some of the intensity of color and suppleness of the pure fabric.

THE JACQUARD AND DOBBY WEAVES. These are the weaves that allow beautiful floral designs or elaborate figures to be woven into a fabric, and the crests and names of fancy hotels to be woven into bathmats. The more important fabrics of these weaves include:

Cotton: damask, terry cloth, tapestry

Silk: damask, brocade tapestry, lamé

Linen: damask

Wool: damask, brocatelle, tapestry (cavalry twill is dobby weave)

Rayon: damask, brocade, brocatelle, lamé

There are other methods for making cloth, aside from weaving, which deserve some mention.

Knitting is probably the most familiar of these processes, since everyone has at least

one friend or relative who knits. A knitted fabric is composed with two needles and one or more yarns to form a series of connecting loops that support one another like a chain.

Crocheting is another familiar method whereby, using just one needle or hook, a chain of loops is formed from a single yarn.

The process by which fibers are matted together by heat, steam, and pressure to form a fabric is called felting. Felt is mainly used for hats.

Knotting (or netting) is the method by which an openwork fabric or net is formed by tying yarns together where they cross one another.

Braiding is the interlacing of three or more yarns or strips of cloth over and under one another. Its most common uses are for trims on garments, and for belts and rugs.

In bonding, fibers are pressed into thin sheets or webs that are held together by adhesive or plastic, and in laminating, several layers of cloth are held together by adhesives. Bonded and laminated fabrics lack the porous quality of most other cloths.

With some background on the weaves and on the fabrics they produce, you will better understand what fabrics to buy. If a saleswoman suggests a crepe dress, for instance, you will know to ask whether it is silk, cotton, or rayon, and you may not mind paying a little more for the superior durability and longevity of silk. You will know that if a label says that a garment is bonded, it will be less porous than a woven fabric; it will be stiff and less natural because it does not breathe well. You will know that it is harder to remove a stain from a skirt made from a ridged twill fabric such as gabar-

Fine knit fabrics such as this one drape beautifully, move well, and are generally flattering to the body.

dine than from a skirt in a plain fabric with no ridges, such as challis, poplin, or chambray. Now let us consider the qualities of various fibers that make up yarn.

There are four major natural fibers: two animal—wool and silk, and two vegetable—linen and cotton. There are also a multitude of synthetics and synthetic blends. We will take them one at a time.

SILK

A product of the industrious silkworm, silk was a favorite of European royalty as far back as the tenth century. It has always been considered a luxury fabric and has always been expensive. In the third century A.D. one pound of silk was worth one pound of gold.

Silk has many good qualities that make it an appealing choice for apparel:

☐ It takes to dye incredibly well. Hence it affords a huge variety of exciting colors to choose from.

☐ Because it holds heat near the body, it is a wonderfully warm and lightweight winter fabric. Yet when woven of very fine yarns in open weaves, it is also cool for summer.

☐ While silk feels delightful next to the skin and looks aristocratic and delicate, it is a remarkably strong, durable fabric.

☐ Because of the elasticity of the fibers, silk garments keep their shape well. (Synthetics, on the other hand, do not.)

☐ Silk can absorb a great deal of moisture and still feel dry.

Silk comes in a variety of textures, owing not only to the different type yarns from which it is made, but also to the fact that there are two distinct varieties of silkworms—wild and cultivated. The fibers of the wild silkworm in their original state are a different color from those

Bold and appealing colors are readily available in silk, a fabric with a natural affinity to dye.

of a cultivated silkworm, and have a coarse, hard texture. Thus fabrics made from wild silk (known as tussah) have a rough, bumpy surface and tend to lack the luster of a smooth, shiny, cultivated silk.

Different silk yarns produce various kinds of silks. The ones that you are most likely to run across are:

Raw silk, which is silk that is wound directly from several cocoons. Since this fabric skips several refining processes, it lacks the luster of fine, reeled silk. It is also less expensive.

Spun silk is made from silk waste (tangled fibers from the outside of the cocoon), and it too is not as strong or lustrous as reeled silk. It has a linty, cottony feeling and is probably the least expensive silk.

The term *pure silk* means that the silk contains no weighting (a treatment that makes the silk feel heavier and reduces its durability). Taffeta is a good example of weighted silk. If a silk is weighted, it must, by law, state so on the label.

The only possible drawbacks to silk are its cost and care: silk should be dry-cleaned and, unfortunately, it is still one of the most expensive fabrics around. I do, however, still feel a few silk items are a worthwhile investment, especially if they are nontrendy classics. I have silk shirts that I have worn for years and that are still in excellent condition. If you don't think that silk fits into your life-style, but you like the look and feel of it, give the new blends a try. They look great—but I can't vouch for their durability.

LINEN

The first recorded material woven by man, linen dates back about 10,000 years to the Neolithic age. Fine linens served as the burial

Silk fabrics have a special luster, and a softness that makes them feel wonderful next to the skin.

shrouds of the Egyptian pharaohs and were the most important textile of biblical times.

Linen is still being produced today and should be respected, if not solely for its age and tenacity, for its many fine qualities. Good linen is durable, soil resistant, washable, cool, absorbent, and good looking—and it improves with age. All in all it is a winning fabric, despite a few drawbacks. Because the high cost of producing and manufacturing fine linen is passed on to the consumer, pure linen garments are expensive. On the other hand, quality linens will outlast almost any other fabric, which in the long run helps equalize the cost.

Because linen is inelastic, it is quick to wrinkle, even when treated for crease resistance. This may or may not be considered a problem, depending on your personal taste. I personally like the look of a wrinkled white linen summer suit (and the images of Casablanca or Marcello Mastroianni it conjures up).

Certain labels are synonymous with fine linen. Moygashel is probably the best known, and represents excellent-quality, 100 percent pure imported Irish linen. Other quality labels include Irish Linen, McBratney, Yorkflax, and Meadow Bleach. Most fine-quality linen fabrics are imported from Northern Ireland, where the making of linen fabric goes back 1,500 years and the workmanship is unparalleled. Although Belgium produces the highest-grade flax (the plant from which linen is derived), most of it is sent to Ireland to be made into cloth.

The Federal Trade Commission has established certain rules for manufacturers that are a great aid to the consumer in determining the quality of linen garments. To be called a linen product an article must consist of at least 50 percent pure linen, and all other fiber contents must be listed in order of weight predominance. If other fibers make up less than 5 percent of the fabric, the term *other fibers* or *mis-*

cellaneous fibers may be used. If an article looks like linen—has a linen finish—but contains no linen, it must be so stated on the label or tag.

With these guidelines in mind, if you do decide to incorporate linen into your wardrobe, you will have a pretty good idea of what you'll be buying.

WOOL

Wool is comfortable, resilient, and durable. It is naturally water repellent and because it prevents heat loss by the body, it is also incredibly warm.

The Wool Products Labeling Act requires that wool apparel have labels indicating the percentage of nonwool fibers they contain, preferably in order of predominance, if these fibers make up more than 5 percent of the total fabric weight. If the nonwool fiber content is less than 5 percent, the label need only say "other fibers." Hence a label might read "50% wool, 45% cotton, 5% other fibers." The term *virgin wool* means that the wool fabric is not constructed from any wastes of wool processing, but is newly processed for the particular fabric.

Wool is derived from the fleece of sheep, with the exception of the so-called specialty fibers, which include the following: mohair, vicuña, alpaca, cashmere, and camel hair. All but camel hair are derived from various species of goats.

This range of outfits shows how one fabric—linen—lends itself to a variety of looks.

A classic tweed (right) *and an effective match of supple suede and shiny leather* (left).

72

Well-designed cottons are available in an array of striking colors.

COTTON

For my money, cotton is king. It is reasonably priced, comfortable in any season, durable, washable, and good looking. Past complaints about cotton—shrinkage, fading, and creasing, have all been remedied by new treatments and finishes. One treatment in particular, mercerizing, gives cotton fabrics some very definite advantages. It makes them stronger, more pliable, more lustrous, more absorbent, and gives them greater affinity for dye, allowing for the great array of bright colors available today. To my mind, cotton is one of the most practical, versatile, wonderful fabrics on the market.

RAYON AND ACETATE

Rayon and acetate were the first synthetics, but because they are both rebuilt from cellulose (which is derived from natural sources—wood pulp and cotton linters), they are, in fact, not true synthetics since they do not have a completely chemical base. As a result, they breathe better than true synthetics. (Acetate less so, since it is combined with acetic acid and is thus a vegetable *and* chemical fiber.)

When rayon was first made in Paris in 1884, it greatly resembled silk and was referred to as artificial silk for many years. The generic term *rayon* was accepted in 1924 for all artificial silks and was thought to be an appropriate and descriptive name since the then lustrous rayon reflected the *rays* of the sun.

Today rayon no longer solely resembles silk. Various treatments and manufacturing methods allow it to simulate different textures of wool, linen, and cotton as well.

As with the natural fibers, there are good, medium, and poor grades of rayon. Needless to say, the grades are not indicated on labels, so you have to go by the way they look and feel. Rayon is an economical and cool fabric. Some rayons lack elasticity and may bag in spots or separate at the seams. It is a good idea to tug a rayon garment gently at the seams to test the slippage. Many antique rayon garments should have their seams reinforced before wearing to be safe.

SYNTHETICS

Synthetics were designed to simulate the natural fibers. Acrylic, polyester, and nylon are generic names. Acrylic was designed to simulate wool, polyester to simulate cotton, and nylon to simulate silk. Within these three divisions each textile company has trade names. DuPont, for instance, has Dacron polyester, Orlon, Antron, acrylic, and Qiana nylon, to name only a few.

Since synthetics are created in the test tube from chemical compounds, they can be made in great quantities, which lowers their cost considerably in comparison to the natural fibers. This is one of their biggest advantages. The other advantage is their easy care and maintenance. Their drawbacks include the fact that synthetic fibers don't breathe and are often far less comfortable than the natural fibers. Wearing a synthetic garment is often akin to wearing a piece of plastic, and synthetics have a lot of static electricity. Durability is another problem—the fabrics often pill (form little balls on their surface), and some synthetics tend to lose their shape after continued use. The loss of shape creates another disadvan-

STAIN REMOVAL

THE BASICS

□ *Don't rub stains. Blot them with a clean white cloth, and place another cloth underneath to absorb the grime.*

□ *Always apply cleaning fluids to the side of the fabric worn on the inside.*

□ *Nonwashable garments with stains should go post haste to a reliable dry cleaner. Remember to tell him the cause of the stain.*

□ *For quick home doctoring, your fabric medicine chest should include carbon tetrachloride (lighting fluid will do), a bleach—hydrogen peroxide or Clorox (not to be used on dyed goods), ammonia, turpentine, and a good presoak-type detergent.*

WHAT TO DO ABOUT COMMON STAINS

Blood. *Soak in cool water with a little table salt added. Then wash with a gentle soap in warm water.*

Coffee/tea/chocolate. *Pour boiling water through the stained portion of the cloth. Then soak in warm water and a good presoak detergent.*

Chewing gum. *Scrape off excess with a dull knife and wipe gently with carbon tetrachloride.*

Grease. *Place a clean white cloth under the stain. Apply carbon tetracarbon or Carbona to the wrong side of the fabric. Wash in hot water.*

Grass. *Apply ammonia and cold water directly to the stain. Soak overnight in a good presoak.*

Perspiration. *Wash in hot water. Bleach if necessary. (Do not bleach dyed garments.)*

Mildew. *Wash in strong detergent and hot water. Hang in the sun. Use bleach if fabric allows.*

Cream and milk. *Wash immediately with cool water.*

Fruit. *Most fruit stains can be removed with boiling water. If the stain is very stubborn, try an ammonia/water solution.*

Paint. *Place white cloth under the stain. Blot the wrong side of the fabric with turpentine. Soak in warm water.*

tage, one of aesthetics—an unsightly bagging at the knees and elbows.

There are various grades of synthetics, just as there are different grades of rayons and the natural fibers. Because of the improved qualities of today's synthetic fabrics, they are presently being used for high-priced garments as well as lower-priced lines. We have gone beyond the days when these fibers should conjure up images of tacky doubleknit suits.

Many top designers are currently using synthetics. Fernando Sanchez has created wonderful lingerie and loungewear from synthetic blends. Joan Sibley uses man-made fibers for elegant evening clothes, and Norma Kamali's designs are almost entirely made of synthetic fabrics.

Every year brings new advances in the quality of synthetics, and, when all is said and done, these fabrics have an indisputably valid and important place in today's world. With the accelerating growth in world population, it would eventually become impossible to clothe everyone in natural fibers.

The important things to consider with your choice of fabrics are their uses within your wardrobe, your comfort requirements, and your general life-style and budget. Some people feel trapped in a layer of polyester, others live in it. Some people who travel a lot find wrinklefree synthetics a godsend; others aren't bothered by a few creases, or carry an iron with them. If budget is a priority, you

A woman should never wear anything she can't do the mambo in.
BETSY GONZALES

might try a mixture of natural and synthetic fibers, and keep the cool natural fibers near your skin. For instance, wear an Orlon cardigan over a soft cashmere turtleneck, or pair a cotton shirt with a Dacron/cotton blend summer jacket.

Another consideration is how well a fabric works with your body type—make sure that you assess its weight and bulk in relation to yours. If you are a small woman, beware of extremely bulky fabrics. A small woman would get lost in a piece of clothing made of a fabric that is too heavy—such as an Irish fisherman's knit sweater or a heavy tweed jacket. A very heavy woman should be careful of extra bulk too; she needn't add even more weight to her appearance. She should also avoid fabrics that are especially lightweight and allow details of the flesh to show through.

Remember, too, that fabric quality is a good part of your fashion statement. There is no doubt that a 100 percent imported linen suit will create a very different impression from one of the same design in 100 percent polyester. Careful attention to fabric quality and texture can make the difference between an ordinary outfit and a really stunning fashion look.

ESSENTIALS

SHOES, STOCKINGS, AND HANDBAGS

No matter what clothing styles you prefer, accessories should play an important part in shaping and defining your wardrobe. They are not mere accompaniments to the perfect skirt, pair of slacks, or dress, but essential components of your total look. The right accessory can be the focal point of an entire outfit, can renew last season's worn-out sweater or blouse, can add a stunning accent to a simply styled jacket or coat.

When you are selecting your accessories, you will undoubtedly be guided by your own personal needs and taste, but this is one area where you should try to remain somewhat flexible in your choices. It is possible to experiment and even make mistakes with accessories, without risking high-stake losses.

As you read through the next two chapters, keep in mind that many of the ideas can be adapted or modified to fit your personality and your life-style. In addition to recommendations for the kinds of shoes, handbags, scarves, belts, and other accessories that you will want to include in your wardrobe for work or for other formal daytime activities and elegant evenings on the town, I have offered suggestions for more playful, whimsical accessories that can be part of your leisure-time wardrobe, or your wardrobe for work if your job is in an informal environment. Do not discard any concepts simply because you haven't tried them before or because they seem too different. That would be defeating the purpose of this book.

SHOES AND BOOTS

These basic accessories should, above all, be comfortable. But comfort need not negate fashion. (At the 1978 Coty Awards, designer Perry Ellis injected some humor by teaming up one of his fur-coat designs with white tennis shoes and gym socks.) If it ever came down to making a choice between comfortable shoes or uncomfortable fashionable shoes, there would be no contest. Comfort would win hands down. If I'm not comfortable, I get grouchy, and that's no fun. Due to my hedonistic tendencies, I keep my shoe wardrobe to a minimum. I like to break in a pair of shoes and wear them as long as they hold together, look presentable, and are compatible with the weather conditions. It's embarrassing to admit, but last year I even wore my favorite multicolored, multi-layered rubber flip-flops with socks, till my toes felt a chill. They were so incredibly comfortable I just couldn't give them up. I am, undeniably, a bit eccentric in the shoe department. But I grew up in Florida where my feet got used to open, easy living. I've only recently come to terms with the necessity of encasing them in leather every once in a while, and I'm still not ecstatic about it.

However, it's easy for me to get away with my eccentricities, and even appear chic by being unchic, because of my environment. Living in New York is itself a factor. New York is a cosmopolitan city where the unusual is commonplace, and one's idiosyncracies are hardly noticed. And there is an incredibly loose dress code that prevails inside the fashion business. Most likely it's because we are so saturated with the serious business side of fashion that we create a sort of nonfashion fashion for ourselves. Everybody I work with pretty much dresses for comfort and practicality during the working hours.

It is necessary, however, to present a

Your shoes should echo the mood of your clothing. The sporty, sophisticated spectator pumps (above) *and chic strappy sandals* (below) *are perfect complements to these outfits.*

more serious, less flippant attitude if your everyday environment is conservative or somewhat formal. You want to feel comfortable mentally as well as physically.

What basic shoes do you need in your wardrobe?

Let us first consider what you will need if you work in a somewhat traditional professional environment.

SHOES FOR THE WORKING HOURS. Aside from the number-one prerequisite of comfort, there are two things to keep in mind when selecting your shoes for work. The first is that they should complement the mood and feeling of your wardrobe. If your clothes tend to be on the tailored side, so should your shoes. A spectator pump or a walking shoe, for instance, would be compatible with a tailored suit. If your wardrobe has a softer theme to it, your shoe style should be more delicate—perhaps a sling-back, open-toed shoe, or sandal.

The color of the shoe is, of course, important. But the shape is of equal importance. A deep tan, nubby tweed suit and a burgundy walking shoe would be a good match. But the style would be too heavy for a silk dress of the same color.

The second thing to keep in mind is that the shoe should complement your leg. There are a few shoe shapes and styles that are risks

These shoe designs by Susan Bennis and Warren Edwards are a sampling of the many styles available in shoes today.

Shoes with a strap across the instep are not always flattering to the leg. But the closer the strap is to skin color, the better the leg will look.

for most everyone. Here are some shoe designs to beware of:

☐ A shoe with a strap across the instep tends to shorten the leg, because the line of the leg is interrupted by the horizontal line of the strap. The closer the shoe is to skin tone, the less risky this design—the strap will then be less obvious and the line less abrupt. The same principle applies to strap styles that fasten around the ankles. I wouldn't advise this type of shoe unless your legs are long, slender, and near perfect.

☐ Shoes with heavy, clunky heels are best avoided. If your legs are heavy, the heels will make them look heavier. If your legs are slender, they will make them look like toothpicks.

☐ Open-toed shoes with closed backs need watching. They can work, and sometimes well. But be sure the toe opening is a good shape. If it only allows the big toe to peek through, or makes the second toe look deformed as it tries to squeeze out into the open air, the toe opening is not a good shape.

☐ Gucci-type walking shoes with a flap or tongue on top can look heavy. Watch the top section (or tongue of the shoe). Generally speaking, a lower tongue that allows more of the instep to show will be more flattering to the leg.

There are also some shoe shapes that are flattering to most everyone. The classic Chanel sling-back is probably one of the most becoming styles around. Besides being comfortable, its design is every bit as much a fashion eternal as a cashmere turtleneck sweater. A well-designed strap sandal provides another flattering shoe line. And the classic pump is another design that works well. In general, it is safe to say that the less shoe, the better the leg will look.

If you think about these things as you try on various shoe styles, the ideas will become crystal clear. When you shop for shoes that you will eventually be wearing with skirts and dresses, do not wear slacks. It will be too difficult to see how the shoe affects your proportions and leg shape.

A few extra pointers:

▫ A medium-height heel will work for everybody and is the best bet for work. But watch the width of the heel. A fairly narrow heel is most flattering to the leg.

▫ Beware of high heels that can hook you on their good looks alone. They look marvelous when you try them on in the store, but are impossible to walk in on the streets. Handsome high heels lose their appeal when they create an awkward, swaying stride.

▫ Remember color flexibility. While black may be a classic, it can often seem too heavy for an outfit. Other colors can work just as well and add a refreshing new dimension. Consider burgundy, forest green, gunmetal, tan, and even red.

▫ White need not always be matched with white. Again, consider other tones. Beige is a good neutral that blends well with most pale shades. White patent leather shoes have a tendency to look inexpensive no matter what you pay for them.

SHOES FOR EVENING. One to three pairs of shoes should prove quite adequate, unless you are wined and dined every night, or you are an inveterate shoe collector. I find sandals to be the most flattering style of shoe with dressy evening attire. They are feminine, sexy, and keep the leg and foot looking wonderfully bare. A heavy shoe can easily weigh down an outfit. Evening is the time you want to feel more sensual, more feminine, and kind of let

White need not always be paired with white. Try beige shoes for contrast and a softer look.

Bright red shoes and belt show how unexpected accessories can perk up an outfit.

your guard down after a hard, busy day. Although I adore my running shoes, they are not terribly conducive to sensuality. If I wear those at night there is always the possibility I might suddenly feel like sprinting off, leaving my dinner partner utterly bewildered.

BOOTS. If you live in a four-season climate, you'll need from two to four pairs of boots.

1. *A good-looking, fine-quality, stylish leather boot.* If you have doubts about style, check the fashion magazines. You will see a broad range of heel heights and styles that will give you a general idea of what is available. Remember though, it is you who'll be wearing the boots, and not the model. Keep your style and comfort in mind when you make your decisions. Mid-tone colors will go with most anything. (I tend toward tans and burgundies.) Here is one place not to skimp. Quality boots will be costly, but they are worth the investment. Inexpensive boots are generally flimsy, poorly styled, and have a relatively short life. Fine leather boots will take you through a few seasons of fall and mild winter days, and they tend to look even better after they're broken in. Buy a boot you are proud to wear.

2. *A hearty boot for nasty winter days.* Handsome-looking fur-lined snow boots with crepe soles are readily available and can easily be waterproofed with spray silicone. Heavy rubber or crepe soles are important in bad weather for comfort, warmth, and safety.

The initial selection of an outfit is, of course, very important, but the way you accessorize it is what helps you pull it off.
SUZY CHAFFEE

Don't skimp here either. These boots will last many seasons. So buy the best-looking, best-quality, and most comfortable you can find.

3. *Rain boots.* Rain boots are something of a joke. Don't try to get too "fashiony" here. Buy inexpensive practical galoshes. Who cares about high fashion when it's raining cats and dogs? Get funky, be comfortable, and have a good time. You can find great foul-weather boots (and other rain gear) at boating-supply stores. They're fun, inexpensive, and incredibly practical.

4. *Optional purchases.* Hiking boots are a handy staple to have around. They are sporty, and tremendously comfortable in crummy city weather as well as on a mountaintop.

Cowboy boots are perfect if you're feeling Western and want to have a little fun. Janice Dickenson has a prized pair that are electric blue, with white chips, pointed toes, and high heels. "When I wear them," she says, "I feel like showing them off like a proud peacock."

PLAYSHOES. There are many different kinds of casual shoes available, some at a very reasonable cost. A few styles to try are: white Capezio dance shoes, for an attractive alternative to sandals with summer whites; tennis shoes, which will look great with loose-fitting cotton shorts or slacks; Woolworth's canvas sandals, priced at under $5.00, to wear to the beach or for lounging around the pool or patio. The flat Chinese version of the old Mary Jane strapped shoe is inexpensive, comfortable, and makes for an interesting look. Moccasins—fur lined for winter and unlined for summer—have always been one of my favorite casual shoes, and the Sperry Topsider moccasin, with soles designed to grip sailboat decks, comes out ahead in all kinds of weather conditions. Scandinavian clogs have become almost as

Camping boots, clogs, espadrilles, tennis and running shoes are comfortable and practical footgear with a casual look.

much an American classic as the penny loafer. Keep your eyes open for unusual, practical, and fun shoes in dance stores, mail-order catalogues, sporting-good stores, and five-and-tens. You would be surprised at the different varieties that are practically in your own backyard.

TIGHTS AND STOCKINGS

Tights worn with dresses and skirts are a plus in the winter and can add a refreshing touch of color to your outfit. Because they are made of heavier fabric than stockings, they provide extra warmth and can enable you to wear some summer skirts and dresses into early fall. Tights come in a wonderful array of colors—it is easy to find them subtle enough to slip unnoticed behind any desk and bright enough to upstage a bird of paradise.

Stockings (panty hose) are available in a huge variety of tones. There are no hard and fast rules for matching clothes and hose, but I suggest a *slightly* darker tone with an overall darkish look, such as a brown or navy tweed suit, or a black evening dress. I would stay pretty close to natural skin tone when choosing stockings to go with any of the medium-value colors, such as red, light gray, natural tan. If your legs are very pale, you can give them a slight panty-hose tan. But unless you especially want to call attention to your legs, I don't advise dark hose with light garments; this very rarely works well.

Patterned hose can sometimes add an interesting accent. The trick is to make sure they are in keeping with your outfit. For instance, a light, delicate dress requires a more delicately patterned hose than a tweed skirt and walking shoe. In all cases, the shoes and hose should be more or less in the same tone, to avoid making your legs and feet the focal point of your outfit.

Some oddities to stay away from include *black fish-net stockings*, unless you're doing *Moulin Rouge* in summer stock or looking for something a little different or naughty to hang on your fireplace instead of traditional Christmas stockings, and the nylon copy of the old-fashioned *silk seamed stockings*. They worked very well for Joan Crawford in 1941, but even she had a hard time keeping her seams straight. They are just another passing fad, hardly worth a second thought.

SOCKS AND STOCKINGS (FOR FUN)

Socks are an often ignored fun accessory. There are antique socks, multicolored striped socks, patterned socks, polka-dot socks, Argyle socks, you name it, and they are out there for the choosing. Socks are an inexpensive fashion pick-me-up.

As an extra bonus, socks can serve as a convenient carryall when you don't feel like

Stockings in a subtle pattern introduce a new texture and add polish to your look.

toting a bag. My trusty socks have easily managed a pack of cigarettes, keys, lip gloss, small compact, and a tortoise-shell comb. If I have a particularly heavy load, I might be inclined to wear two pair of socks and pack my goodies between them, for ankle comfort (make sure the top of the sock is made with strong elastic).

Socks also help in the creation of a total look:

1. *Argyle socks* worn with loafers mix well with tweeds, flannels, and wools for a classic campus look.

2. *White socks* with flat leather sandals can create a European schoolgirl look.

3. *Heavy wool socks* are a natural with hiking boots and can serve as toppers rolled over the top of any sporting boot. They help keep your pant bottoms tucked against your leg when hiking and biking and can add to a general active-sport look. This look is most successful when worn while actually engaging in sports activities. Exercise is chic.

HANDBAGS

Convenience is the key word in bags today. The *hand*bags of yesterday are the *hand*bags of today—practical, functional pouches that hang from shoulders, waists, and necks. Today's fashion-conscious woman is unencumbered, free to move on to the business "at hand."

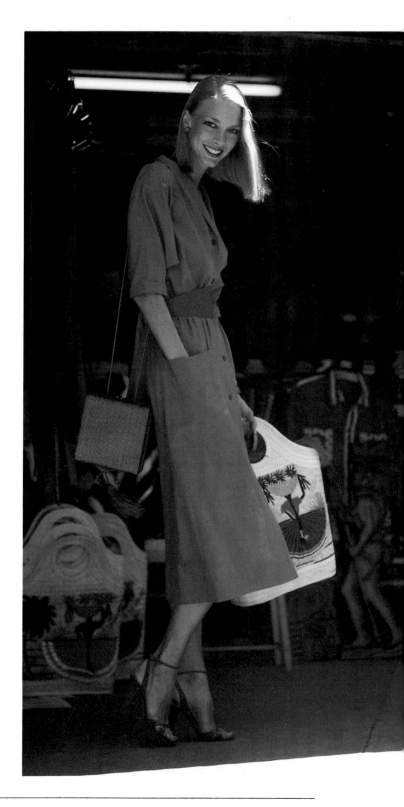

Your handbag should suit your lifestyle. If you don't have much to carry, try a trim shape like this—with a dash of color.

DAYTIME. Using a different bag every day is not convenient, so forget the constant juggling of possessions from one satchel to another. It is no longer necessary. The days of mandatory matching of shoes and bags have thankfully gone the way of white gloves and Merry Widow corsets. When styling for fashion ads I actually make a conscious effort to blend the shoe and bag colors and textures, rather than match them perfectly. I find that it makes for a more contemporary and sophisticated fashion look. Think of it in terms of coordinating rather than matching. If your shoes complement your ensemble and your bag does likewise, the entire outfit will work together. Colors such as natural leather, deep burgundy, mahogany, and gray are good complements to the earth tones, and light tan and natural straw work well with pale tones.

A handbag should do two things. Number one, its style should meet your needs. Some of you need a bag that is roomy, others require a bag that is compartmentalized and well organized, and still others a bag that is lightweight and small. There are plenty of wonderful styles to choose from that will satisfy your personal requirements.

The second job your bag should do for you is add a finish to your fashion look and help define your personal style. Hence it should be in keeping with your clothes, personality, and body type.

If your fashion approach is soft and untailored, you might look best carrying a lightweight unconstructed suede pouch. If you have settled upon a crisp, tailored image for yourself, your bag should be neat and trim, perhaps in a fine-quality, polished leather. A large, floppy, canvas fishing bag would be an obvious contradiction to both these dress styles.

I am now in the third year of a wonderful relationship with an olive green battue shoul-

Americans tend to match too much— they are very conscious about everything matching perfectly. They also tend to overaccessorize—overbelt, overchain, overbracelet. The thing to remember is that you are the one that should be looked at, not what you're wearing.
BILL BLASS

der bag (three-ply heavy nylon, lighter in weight than canvas) that I bought at Hunting World, an expensive New York boutique that caters to the elite sportsman and big game hunter. At the time I made the purchase I was unjustly accused of being a spendthrift. The bag did cost a good deal, but it met all *my* qualifications with flying colors. It is an incredibly well made bag. I've used it, abused it, and re-used it, and it still looks great. Its five separate compartments help keep my disorganization to a minimum, and it's roomy enough to hold my notebooks, camera, and all the other assorted paraphernalia I need. It's strong enough to travel on the back rack of my bicycle, and even comes equipped with an inside clasp for a Swiss army knife. What more could I ask for in a bag? I would not be a bit surprised if, when the time comes, I replace it with an exact duplicate.

What may be the perfect bag for me may not be for you. Clutch bags are the preference of my lawyer friend. She would rather carry one bag than two, and since her work requires a briefcase, the clutch bag is perfect. She slips it in her briefcase and off she goes. And it is the perfect size to take to lunch and meetings.

Another friend of mine carries a smallish shoulder bag and hates big bags. She finds a big bag a nuisance in the office where she works. She can never find any place to put it; it won't fit in her drawer, so the bag is always in the way.

Find the bag that works the best for *you*.

COST AND BODY-TYPE CONSIDERATIONS. Since this bag will be your daily companion, do not compromise on quality. An inexpensive, poorly made bag will make a well-put-together outfit look ordinary. Conversely, a quality bag can upgrade an outfit.

When you carry a bag on your shoulder, it should fall anywhere from mid-hip to just below your armpit. If you are petite, you will not look best with a bag that is too long, and if you are tall, a very short bag will not be most flattering to you. The same goes for very large and small bags on petite and tall people. Body type is not a huge consideration here except in the extremes.

EVENING. For evening and/or leisure activities, two or three small pouches should suffice: one for your casual nights out at the movies or visiting friends, and another one or two for dressier affairs. All should be convenient and workable within the scope of your wardrobe.

If you already own the few evening pouches that you *need* but run across one that is an irresistible knockout, buy it anyway. Anytime you find a very special accessory that fits within your budget—be it a bag, scarf, piece of jewelry, pair of shoes, or what have you—buy it. You will find that these spur-of-the-moment accessory purchases can be lifesavers in times of doubt when you just can't figure out what to wear. The addition of one wonderful new accessory can perk up and give new life to a tired old outfit. Once you begin to trust your instincts and know what you like and don't like, the items you purchase will tend to go together—and it will be a challenge to

make the more unexpected combinations work.

If you are handy with a needle and feel creative, you can make evening bags from any favorite fabric, or even antique napkins; they are sure to be unique. Bags are easy to put together. Almost every pattern book has some good ideas and easy patterns in the back pages.

ON THE ROAD. One last type of bag I feel I must mention is the knapsack. You might identify this indispensable energy saver with mountain climbers and hippies (not a totally unjustified association). But there's a method to their knapsack madness. If you've never worn a knapsack, you'll be amazed at its comfort and practicality. The knapsack slips around both shoulders and is centered on the back. The weight is then evenly distributed on the back. You feel as if you're carrying almost nothing. There's no discomfort and no strain. (You can also sling it over one shoulder when the load is light.) It's a great alternative to heavier shoulder bags on holiday when you might find yourself doing a lot of walking, touring, and buying. They come in good-looking, extremely lightweight nylon, can fold to the size of a large napkin for easy packing, and can carry an incredible amount.

On a past Paris flea-market expedition I was as comfortable as I have ever been. It was wonderful to buy what I wanted without the fear of being burdened down with hundreds of little parcels. The more I purchased, the more my knapsack proved to be a worthy and valuable companion. It's a fabulous carryall for beach paraphernalia as well. If you're planning a holiday, try a knapsack. It probably won't be long before a designer adapts the knapsack into real fashion anyway. They are simply too practical and comfortable to be overlooked.

ACCENTS

BELTS, SCARVES, JEWELRY, HATS, LINGERIE, HAIR, AND MAKEUP

You have just seen what important influence "essentials" can have on your total look. In this chapter, we will have a look at some fashion accents—belts, scarves, hats, and jewelry, with lingerie, hairstyles, and makeup added for good measure. These accessories are the extras that can make dressing truly individual, creative, and fun.

Happily, the sources of many of the more fanciful accessories are limitless, because so many useful items have the potential to become a clothing accessory. If you wrap a yard of a jib line from a sailboat, or a simple hemp rope, around your waist, it's a belt. If you appropriate a fancy fish lure from your husband's tackle box and stick it on your jacket, it's a pin. Hang a seashell around your neck—bingo, a necklace! *Nothing is off-limits. Anything can be used.*

Don't be afraid to use things out of context; forget their original purpose. Objects happened upon in the most unexpected places can, with a quick pirouette of the imagination, be turned into scarves, belts, jewelry, or hair ornaments. There are many unexpected sources of accessories close by. Equestrian supply stores, for example, that supply riders with everything they need, from horse feed to riding jackets, are a veritable storehouse of fashion discoveries. Riding jackets, boots, and Western-style belts with interchangeable buckles are among the more obvious items. Horse bridles of fine braided leather, with silver and copper details, can be made into belts with just a bit of creativity.

I have a wardrobe that's between funky and classic. I have my classic pieces, then I jazz them up a bit so that they're not so predictable that they're boring.
SHELLEY SMITH

Hats, antique fur scarves, bolo ties, Western belts with silver buckles, and cowboy boots are just a sampling of the many accessories that can be found off the beaten track.

I have passed through many a Western store in my day, but it wasn't until I was in Phoenix, Arizona, styling legitimate rodeo stars for Wrangler jean ads that my imagination took hold, and I realized the potentials of the stock Western items that others around me took for granted. While we were shooting pictures in one of the local horse-gear stores, I asked the saleslady if it would be possible for her beltmaker to adjust a few straps, combine my choices of a nose band and martingale, remove a bit from one bridle and replace it with another, and put it all together so that it looked exactly like the two-second sketch I had just badly drawn. There was no doubt that she thought I was absolutely nuts, but after a quick verbal exchange with her boss, she said she would be happy to take care of it.

By the time it was finished, they were all convinced I was, at the very least, eccentric, but a brilliant belt designer nonetheless. I had an incredible belt, almost custom-made, for a mere pittance of what it might have cost had it been predesigned and sold in a boutique or department store. I thought of it first, that's all. And I still receive compliments on the belt today—seven years later. The moral? Keep your eyes open and your imagination finely tuned.

Antique stores, boat-supply stores, sporting-good stores, flower shops, even pet stores (try buckling a few dog or cat collars together) are some untapped sources for accessories that will transform your outfits from ordinary to sublime. Designers are always on the lookout for them; no reason you shouldn't get there first.

In addition to the creative accessories you can put together on your own, you may occasionally want to try one of the numerous fad items that appear each season. But a warning: don't spend a lot of money on faddish doodads that will be in today and out tomorrow. Save your dollars for those classic accessories and garments that will be wearable for a long time and prove your investment worthwhile. Fads are for fun, and they're funny, but it's important to be able to distinguish them from styles. A fad is a T-shirt with your own picture on it, a pair of jeans studded with rhinestones, or shoes with five-inch platforms. Styles last longer than fads and make more of a definite fashion statement. A narrow-lapeled jacket or a wide belt are styles, and though they might not be part of a look that is being promoted for the next season, they can be worn from one season to the next if they are flattering to you. A style can easily become part of *your style*, whereas fads make for too contrived a look on any kind of long-term basis. So treat them in the spirit that they were created—fun while they last.

Nina Blanchard's got the right idea. She suggests: "The only way to deal with fads is to say how much does it cost and can I afford to throw it away in six months. If you can afford fads, they can be fun. But if you have no shoes,

When budget is a consideration, avoid trendy items like these pants. Stick with classic designs that will see you through seasons of wear.

don't buy wedgies with sequins, because it simply isn't a practical thing if you have to go to work. Many women make the mistake of buying something that's on sale, and it generally is on sale precisely because it was a fad and is no longer in style. Then they are stuck with it, and can end up with a closet full of garbage."

The "Annie Hall" look is a perfect example of a fad and can serve to reinforce these admonitions. I was told by Ara Gallant, who knows Diane Keaton well, "The look was Diane's own; it evolved from her individuality. She would wear two dresses or two suits at the same time, or oversized vests, or whatever, and it worked for her. It grew out of the way Diane preferred to look. Her style was 'organically processed.' Women who tried to adopt the entire look for themselves were counterfeit Annie Halls; they were sacrificing their look to keep up with a fad—to be in style. Women who treasured their individuality and were sporting vests or string ties before the look became popular stopped wearing them, so as not to look *faddish*. Susan Blakeley put her vests on the shelf till the fad ran its course; 'When a look becomes someone's trademark, I don't want to wear it. I don't feel special.' "

When shopping, give in to a fad every now and then if one appeals to you. But remember, well-designed, well-made classics will outlive trendy items because of their superior quality and style. A case in point: six years ago I allowed myself a luxury I could little afford at the time (God bless my American Express card), a gold Rolex watch. I had decided that I genuinely needed a versatile, dependable wristwatch—one that wasn't allergic to dishwater, wouldn't balk at sharing my bath or shower, whose accuracy wouldn't be impaired by my unintentional but habitual carelessness and rough treatment, and would plod loyally ahead without being wound and pampered nightly. My decision was made; I was prepared to spend a little extra money for the very best.

Well, the little extra turned out to be rather a substantial amount. Vanity was my downfall. I was on location, working in Bermuda at the time, and had acquired a wonderful bronze color—a tan to be remembered. Anyway, as I was trying on the aluminum watch that I had originally set out to buy, my eye was captivated by the solid-gold version of the same watch. There were no longer any options: the gold harmonized with my new Bermuda tan; the aluminum looked positively shoddy by comparison. Aesthetics, I rationalized, took precedence over money considerations. (The absolute antithesis of my usual security-oriented, deeply ingrained monetary philosophy.) It was a totally refreshing experience, although I'm sure my pulse count was unusually high as I signed my credit-card voucher.

As luck would have it, my first expensive impulse buying proved triumphant in all respects. Not only did my solid-gold Rolex become a minor status symbol within a few years (not necessarily a plus), not only does it fulfill all my life-style requirements in grand style, and not only does it look as good as the day I bought it, but my one favorite piece of jewelry has more than doubled in price. Six years later—no regrets.

Belts can make an outfit. Here are a variety of different styles.

BELTS

There is nobody whose wardrobe could not profit from the addition of a few good-looking belts. They are one of my all-time favorite accessories and make up the major part of my accessory wardrobe. Belts are useful, practical, and handy little fashion staples, and they are usually reasonably priced. A belt alone can change the shape, proportion, drape, or style of your outfit. It can perk up a boring ensemble or update an old one. And these days a lot of belts are designed with small pouches that can serve as convenient totes.

I used to collect belt buckles (one of the main goals of my flea-market expeditions) and make my own belts to go with them. It was fun and easy, and they made super gifts. All you actually have to do is attach a strip of leather or fabric to a buckle and sometimes, depending on the style of buckle, make some small holes for the tongue of the buckle. Very few tools are needed: some Sobo glue and a hole punch are the only essentials for the occasional beltmaker. Over the years I have amassed a variety of rivets, snaps, and tools, but you can create your belts without them.

Some belts are so special that they really make an outfit. I sometimes wear a pair of black slacks, a black blouse, and a black belt with a striking red-beaded Indian buckle that I picked up in Jackson Hole, Wyoming. The color and design of the belt gives the whole outfit a unique flair.

A handsome tan or burgundy leather belt in a narrow to medium width would be a useful addition to almost any wardrobe. There are also many inexpensive novelty belts around that can add a certain flavor to an outfit. One of my favorites is the one-and-one-quarter-inch canvas army belt. It comes in almost all colors, including black, white, red, olive, beige, and navy, and is available at all army-navy stores and many department stores. The belts range in price from one to three dollars and usually come in one size, but they are designed so that they can easily be shortened. Have the salesperson show you how to do it.

Another find are Indian beaded belts (made in Hong Kong, incidentally). Shelley Smith thinks these are "the best buy in America." Most "tourist" cities have a slew of them with the name of the city beaded on the back

Gold accessories add sparkle to this outfit of cream and olive silk.

INVENTIVE ACCESSORY IDEAS—FASHION FOOD FOR THOUGHT

SUZY CHAFFEE

One time a hairdresser chopped off my hair a little more than I wanted—I know that a longer hair look, pulled back from the front into a sort of ponytail, then flowing in the back, is the most flattering to me. Anyway, I no longer had long hair, but I wanted to create the illusion that I did. So I got three beautiful foxtails that were joined together with a string. I tied the string around a comb and stuck the comb over my short stubby ponytail. From a distance people thought I had really long hair, and close up they were just gorgeous foxtails that flattered my face. So I skied in my Bogner whites and my three foxtails. (P.S. That was the year Suzie was voted the best-dressed woman skier.)

SHELLEY SMITH

I like to tie a little something around my neck—nothing as big as a scarf, but something like a very narrow leather cord, a ribbon, or a silk string that might come with a blouse. It's a kind of personal touch that adds interest and doesn't detract from the length of the neck.

PAM SUTHERN

I love flowers. Lots of times I'd buy freesia and wear them at my waist or neck. Little things like this seem to bring your style and personality out. Also I was wearing kimonos long before most people discovered them. I'd match them up with pants and wear them out to dinner or disco. They usually cost no more than twenty dollars, and they were super, a perfect complement to my flower phase.

YASMINE

I used to live in India and I learned some terrific ways of wrapping, pleating, and tucking fabrics. I make a lot of dresses out of cloth just by wrapping it, or twisting it and wearing it over one shoulder. These dresses feel great and look wonderful. One time I found this really beautiful fabric, so I just folded it in two and cut a hole in the middle for the head. It kind of drapes down over the arms. Since it's completely open on the sides, I belt it. You can still see into the

sides, but it's very sexy. Or I could wear very snug, form-fitting pants under it. It's great, and it falls wonderfully in graceful pleats.

PAT CLEVELAND

I have a drawer just for accessories. Anything I find that I think I can attach to my clothing I toss into the drawer. I may not use it immediately, but eventually it'll pop into my mind. There are so many accessory potentials around. You can go to the five-and-ten and buy a hair comb, then put some kind of decoration on it and slip it into your hair. Hair combs are one of the most feminine accessories in the world.

I love toy pins. I have a whole collection of them—tigers, clowns, little faces. I buy them any time I see an outstanding one. I wear them on my hats, shirts, jackets, sweaters, pants.

Sometimes I even attach them to my shoes.

Everything is worthy of consideration. In a secondhand store I found some fifty-cent sparkly green pom-poms that attach to your shoes. I wore them New Year's Eve and they really added some pizazz to my outfit. It's great to have little toys like these. They're fun, inexpensive, and are amazingly effective in creating an individual look.

KIM BASSINGER

I really have a good time making jewelry from the unexpected, from things I just run across. I have made necklaces and belts from hardware-store bolts, shells, and sand dollars that I've found on the beach, tiny pinecones, and even walnut shells. One time I painted a half of a walnut shell with silver and gold, made a tiny hole in the top, and attached it to an old silver chain. It was a knockout; people kept asking me where I got it. I loved telling them I made it, and it cost me less than a dollar. You don't have to spend a lot of money to look chic; you just have to be a little clever.

JANICE DICKENSON

I wear everything. I love creating different things to wear. If I'm wearing something sort of Indian, I'll stick a piece of bamboo in my hair. I wear feathers, punk jewelry. To me, nothing is unwearable.

(although they come without the advertising too). I love collecting these belts—I have some from Bermuda, Wyoming, Arizona, Florida. They come in all colors and go with everything. Price range: three to five dollars.

When vacationing, always keep your eyes peeled for local creations in leather, straw, or whatever. There are not only bargains to be found in belts, but in bags, sandals, jewelry, shawls, hats, and all kinds of clothing.

Almost any body type is compatible with belts. It is simply a matter of finding the right belt style for you and learning how to wear it. Let us consider a few different body types:

THE RENOIR. Narrow- to medium-width belts (1/2″ to 1″) would be the best. Unless you are exceptionally long waisted, a wide belt or a belt worn high on the waist would tend to overemphasize your generous bosom. It is best to wear your belt at the waist or slightly below.

THE ATHLETE. Since there is a tendency in this body type to accumulate extra weight around the midriff, many women of this build never even consider incorporating belts into their wardrobe—they do not want to bring attention to what they consider their "no-waist." In principle this is a correct assumption. But with all rules there are exceptions.

As we discussed in the proportion chapter, a thick waist can easily be masked with vests, cardigans, and other sweaters and tops that cover each side of the midriff. If you were to wear a belt the same color as the bottom half of your ensemble, that had a buckle of vertical design, you would in fact be visually lengthening your body, as well as adding an interesting fashion touch.

THE PEAR. Belts are fine for you too. But remember you want to balance your narrow torso and your broad hips. A very wide belt would only emphasize the proportional discrepancy. Stick to narrow and medium belts worn at the waistline—a belt worn on the hips would highlight their dimensions.

THE BULGE. Within this body type it is the long-waisted/short-waisted variable that can limit your choice of belts. If you are long waisted, you have no problem with belts—wide or narrow—and can wear any of the fabulous wide wrap belts that are readily available, or even two narrow belts together. If you are short waisted, stick to narrow to medium widths. It is not advisable for this body type to wear belts too low on the hips, as this would tend to direct the eye to the thigh bulge.

SCARVES

Scarves are useful for a number of reasons:

1. They can add a needed touch of color or contrast to make an outfit more interesting.

2. They can fill in empty necklines and change the shape of existing ones.

3. They can deflect attention from a trouble spot and accent a pretty face.

4. They can help keep your body warm on a chilly day.

5. They can pinch hit as bikini tops, belts, turbans, hairbands, or, if you are really in a jam, you can wrap up all your worldly possessions in one, tie it on a stick, and hit the road like Huck Finn.

Scarves are an inexpensive and easy way to add a personal touch to your fashion. Apollonia wound two together as a headband to round out a peasant look.

Scarves come in a variety of shapes, sizes, and textures, and it is these factors, combined with your body type, wardrobe needs, and individual style that will ultimately determine their use within your wardrobe.

To be most effective and contribute successfully to a particular ensemble, a scarf should look natural and feel comfortable. Constant readjusting and fidgeting are annoying distractions in any situation. It is not unusual to pin or double-edge-tape a scarf into a set position for photography, and you can apply these devices to your own scarves. But the easiest way to assimilate scarves into your wardrobe and to get the most from what they have to offer is to wear them in a loose and easy style. Try to tie or drape them so that no matter how they shift, they will still look good. For this reason I don't recommend tying scarves around the neck, cowboy-bandana style. Although I frequently use this style for photographs, it is a hard one to carry off unless you are a veteran scarf wearer. It is a stiff, confining look that tends to seem too studied, too styled.

Silk scarves are wonderful. But this is an area where you can easily substitute a less expensive synthetic blend. Since scarves only cover a very small portion of the body, you will not have much of a problem if the synthetic fabric you choose does not breathe well. And it is actually easier to find wonderful, subtle, sophisticated printed scarves in delicate synthetics than in silk. There are also lovely scarves available in light cotton muslins that are perfect for summer. Chiffon is another texture option in scarves, but because there are very few contemporary fashion looks that it complements, I would most often rule chiffon out.

Five ways to wear a narrow oblong scarf.

Five ways to wear a medium-sized square scarf.

As with belts, scarves are compatible with any body type, depending on the way that they are worn. Simply remember your proportional best bets. If you are small, stay away from scarves that are too bulky or overpowering. If your neck is short, wear a scarf over your shirt instead of under, or drape a very narrow scarf loosely around your neck. If you have sloping or wide shoulders, avoid extra-wide scarves.

Of all scarf shapes and sizes, I find long, oblong scarves to be the most versatile. They can be worn in a huge variety of ways, and their shape will even allow two to be tied together. On this page you will see some examples of different modes of tying scarves. Try some of these possibilities, but don't be afraid to experiment and discover some ways of your own invention.

JEWELRY

Jewelry is one of fashion's most personal and subjective accessories, one that can say a lot about the wearer. A piece of jewelry given to you by your favorite Aunt Carrie or an old paramour, or that was purchased during that memorable vacation of '64, steps out of the realm of fashion. Though it may still be termed an accessory, it simply doesn't play by the same fashion rules. It is not necessarily fashionable or unfashionable, rather it's the symbol of a memory. It doesn't matter if you wear diamonds and jeans or rubies and lace, wear your "sentimental" jewelry with whatever you like—if you truly love a piece of jewelry and if it makes you feel good, it will work.

Aside from the nostalgic, I stick to my premise of no restrictions. There is, for in-

stance, no such thing as too much or too little jewelry—within reason, of course. Wilhelmina wears a slew of bracelets, and they look great on her ("I wear so many bracelets sometimes you can hear me coming a mile away"). I, on the other hand, would feel uncomfortable, both mentally and physically, similarly bedecked. I am most comfortable with almost no jewelry. It is simply a matter of individual taste and style.

But even though there are no rules, I don't want to leave you completely directionless. Here are a few pointers to consider:

1. *Less is more.* When in doubt, leave it out. An editor friend of mine who tends toward heavy-duty accessorizing set herself a hard and fast rule: when she is finished "getting her act together," she goes to the mirror and removes one accessory. It is a good idea if you have a tendency to overaccessorize.

2. Wear any favorite knickknacks, but do not treat them as serious fashion statements. Have fun with them. Wear them in a light, jovial spirit. Fasten them where they are not expected or wear them out of context, such as a rhinestone brooch on a denim jacket lapel.

3. Dangling, flashy, extra-large earrings are tacky. Avoid them.

4. Do not let your jewelry overwhelm you. Watch for appropriate proportions. Do not, for instance, wear a necklace so big that your neck disappears. This goes for earrings, bracelets, and rings as well. Over the years I've noticed that no matter how many pairs of earrings I

Overaccessorizing is a common pitfall. Often all that's needed is a small hair ornament (above) *or a few simple bracelets* (below).

A delicate flower at the neck adds a touch of romance to this simple but daring dress.

bring to a booking, I end up using small gold or silver—or lately tiny diamond—studs. Anything large tends to dominate the face, and colored earrings can often blend in with hair, skin, or collars and lose their effect. A small gold stud can add an extra spark without being overpowering.

Marilyn Monroe never wore jewelry. She wanted nothing to interfere with her look. In fact, there's a rather amusing story about this. When Frank Sinatra once gave her some magnificent diamond and emerald earrings, she put them on and asked her secretary if she liked them. Her secretary told her they were fantastic. She said she "couldn't take her eyes off them." "What do you mean?" asked Marilyn. "I mean, they're the first thing I see when I look at you" was the reply. "They're yours," said Marilyn. The story ends with a very happy secretary. There is no reply on record from Sinatra.

5. You can use certain pieces of jewelry to help create a line or to improve upon an existing one. For example, if the buttons on a favorite blouse are awkwardly placed, so that when two buttons are left open the neckline is too high and with three undone it's too low, there are a few ways jewelry can come to the rescue. You can wear a string of pearls or beads over the blouse and knot them to fall between the second and third button to prevent the blouse from opening too far. The currently popular Western accessory, the bolo tie (a thin string tie held in place with a decorative loop), can serve the same purpose, or a handsome pin or delicate pierced earring can be used as a makeshift in-between button.

Pierced earrings are actually one of my favorite multipurpose jewelry items (and I don't even have pierced ears). Besides serving as substitute buttons, they can be used to keep sleeves that have been rolled up from falling down, or used to hold scarves in place.

Your jewelry box is full of possibilities— an old ring can be worn as a scarf loop, or an interesting cufflink as a lapel buttonhole filler. These are all examples of accessories that are being used for purposes other than those for which they were originally designed. I hope you will take them as a starting point and come up with some inspiring creations of your own.

The current jewelry trend seems inclined

toward special favorite pieces that are worn more or less constantly:

□ Sunny Griffen wore a small gold star around her neck for three years; she never took it off. Avon got so many letters inquiring where it could be purchased that they finally copied it, called it "the Sunny Star" after their spokeswoman, and sold more than eight million of them.

□ Barbara Feldon has one favorite delicate gold chain and three favored items of sentimental value that she alternately hangs on it. Her pendants are a blue Fabergé egg, an antique key from a castle in England, and a tiny piece of coral from Tahiti. She also has one pair of gold-hoop earrings that she always wears, and that's it.

□ Eileen Ford wears her favorite string of pearls every day.

□ Apollonia has a few favorites: her silver Indian marriage belt and a number of small rings that are symbolically valuable to her.

□ Suzie Coeleho wears her antique diamond pendant and diamond-stud earrings with everything, even her green running shorts and blue running shoes. (She looks great.)

To end with an exception to all the above women: Jerry Hall is one who collects jewelry. Her philosophy is that "jewelry is an investment. If you are going to invest, you should invest in something fun. Who wants to invest in stocks and bonds? You never see them, and you don't get any fun out of them."

HATS

There was a time not long ago when having a good milliner was as important as having a good doctor. A well-dressed woman was a woman in a hat. If you look back over the photographs of the continuing saga of Jacqueline

Hats can be classic or sporty, or a dramatic topping for fantasy fashions. They will highlight the mood of your outfit.

Kennedy Onassis, it is easy to see when hats stopped being a serious and compulsory part of a total fashionable look. In the mid-sixties the best-dressed Mrs. Onassis hung up her pillbox hat and opted for a loose, free coiffure.

Today hats are back in the picture, but not as a symbol of fashion status quo. Hats today should be worn like the clothes of today, with fun and a carefree spirit. And the hats you wear should complement your personality. Sometimes a hat will suit a personality so well that it becomes a personal trademark—as in the case of many movie and TV detectives, from Humphrey Bogart as Sam Spade to Telly Savalas as Kojak. And until recent times Bella Abzug was never seen without her trademark atop her head.

Most often it's not so much the hat itself that is responsible for this instant association, but rather the way that it is worn. And that's the trick with hats—feeling so comfortable and natural in them that they are almost a part of you. Do that and you're a successful hat wearer.

If you are going to wear any hats these days, other than an inconspicuous winter warmer, prepare yourself for the inevitable comments. The more personality and pizazz the hat has, the more likely the comments. People just aren't used to seeing hats as part of a fashion look anymore, except in the still wild West. To prove my point, I called on my friend

I love hats, I have millions of them, but I never wear them. I buy them and try to wear them, but I always end up taking them off. I'm not ready for hats. I always feel that people are staring at me when I wear hats.

JERRY HALL

Hats are great. I wear them all the time—sailor hats, workmen's hats, old felt hats in the winter, ski caps, fur caps—they're wonderful. I love my black derby—it's been one of my trademarks. Older men think it's fantastic, and cabdrivers too.

JANICE DICKENSON

Betsy Cameron, who possesses a far-ranging hat collection and has no qualms about wearing any one of them. Together we planned a quick, easy experiment in the name of fashion science. Betsy donned her most conservative cowboy hat, I tucked my tape recorder in my army-jacket pocket, and we set off for a quick stroll up Madison Avenue. The results bore out my claim.

Within one block the comments started. "You girls from Mineral Springs?" asked a Wall Street type with his attaché case clasped in his hand. "Good-looking hat you got there," remarked an appealing chap in tweed blazer

Some hats won't go unnoticed on city streets.

and blue jeans. And so it went. "Like your hat." "You girls just get into town or just leaving?" "Where did ya get that hat? Colorado?" During our fifteen-minute, seven-block stroll we chalked up six genuine cowboy hat remarks, and that's discounting the "Hey, cowboy!" and "Where's your horse?" comments from the local construction workers (who would whistle at a cockroach if it wore high heels).

Don't let me discourage you from wearing hats. They can add polish or wit to your look. My point is simply that there must be a genuine harmony between your hat and your personality. Otherwise you better be in good spirits and ready to handle the inevitable comments.

There are far more accessories to discover—gloves, sunglasses and visors, shawls, and leg warmers. All you need do is stay alert: flip through fashion magazines, watch people on the street, look for fashion ideas in movies and on TV, and don't forget that everything out there is a possibility.

LINGERIE—THE HIDDEN ACCESSORY

Although few people are privy to your underwear collection, lingerie is still an important part of fashion, and for large women it is a necessary foundation. But no matter what your size, there are some fashions that deserve special underwear consideration.

Cool, comfortable, lightweight summer slacks in whites and pastels are often somewhat transparent. It would not be advisable to wear them over your flowered underpants. The best choice would be underpants in a color that is close to your skin tone and in a fabric that is relatively sheer without being reveal-

*Examples of the new simple and ele-
gant lingerie.*

ing. Bikinis in a flesh tone would be almost impossible to discern. White, on the other hand, would show through.

Full or half slips are handy liners for clinging or ultra-sheer skirts or dresses.

Sheer blouses and dresses deserve better than serving as a mere veiling for your bra. Nothing looks tackier than a bra revealed under a thin fabric, and this is even less excusable with all the lovely camisoles that are offered in the stores these days.

If you have never really been a lingerie fancier, you should look at some of the attractive, imaginative styles that are currently available in intimate apparel. Loungewear has developed from its rather utilitarian beginnings into an exciting new fashion area. Such designers as Fernando Sanchez and John Kloss have come up with creations that are colorful, comfortable, elegant, and sensual. They can be worn at home for intimate evenings or small gatherings with friends.

There is virtually no limit to what you can spend for a smashing loungewear outfit, but, fortunately, some very attractive designs are presently available at affordable prices. Many department stores offer loungewear at both medium and high-priced cost levels.

*The more you are exposed to beauty
and creativity, the more you will chisel
your mind, yourself, your life-style;
the quality of your life will be
influenced in a very positive manner.*
FERNANDO SANCHEZ

As today's loungewear designs are often close approximations of elegant pants outfits and dresses, many of the proportional best bets and risks that apply to the rest of your wardrobe will apply in this area as well. You will have more flexibility—loungewear is still less constructed than "street clothes"—but stay away from shoulders and waistlines, and tunic, jacket, and hemline lengths that are generally unflattering to you, where they apply.

HAIR

Hair and makeup are mentioned in this chapter because they too are accessories: if your hair and makeup are right for you, they can add a special finish to your overall look. But they can break you if they're off. Heavy, overdone makeup and/or a bouffant hairdo are as deadly as black, clunky shoes worn with a white chiffon dress.

Since fashion is my forte, and hair merely a sideline, most of the information here is compliments of two of my good friends: Suga, who now has a salon at Bergdorf Goodman and is working on a book that promises to offer an all-inclusive look at hair; and Martin Downey, who has been with Revlon and Charles of the Ritz and now freelances for most of the top magazines, fashions ads, and TV commercials.

What are the main considerations when deciding on the right hairstyle?

1. The quality and texture of your hair should be your first consideration. Is it fine, thin, medium, thick, coarse, or naturally straight, wavy, curly, or frizzy?

2. Realistically acknowledge what your hair can do and what you want it to do. Obviously, if you have very fine hair, you cannot wear it like Farrah Fawcett, or if you have very coarse hair, you cannot wear it long and straight. Once you understand your hair, work with it. It's best not to fight it, or you will only have to work harder to maintain the look.

3. What is your life-style? If you live on a sailboat year round and have to conserve fresh water, it would be very inconvenient to have extra-long hair. Or if you work in a very conservative environment, a very trendy or frizzy, bizarre hairdo would be self-defeating.

4. What is your budget? How much can you afford to spend on maintenance? If you have a style that needs trimming every two weeks, its upkeep might be too expensive.

5. What kind of clothes do you wear? Are they classic or trendy? Your hairdo should work in harmony with your overall image. If you wear all the latest "in" things, then your hairstyle can be the latest in thing. If you supplement your classic wardrobe with a few of the latest things, then update your hairdo a bit. The more trend conscious you are about your clothes, the more trend conscious you should be about your hair.

6. What is your face shape? The line of your hair should be flattering to the shape of your face. There are six general face shapes: round, oval, square, diamond, heart, and triangle. Once you know which of these shapes best defines your face, you will know what you want your hairstyle to do for it. If you have a round face, for example, you might want to slenderize it—you would want a style that narrows the lines and that is slightly asymmetrical—and you would avoid any hairdo that would add more fullness to your face. If you have a square face, you will want a style that softens the lines. It is best to find a good hairdresser and work out the problems together.

7. What is your body shape? You want your hairstyle to complement your body. If you have a full, round body, long, straight hair

would look strange on you, and similarly if you are very long and angular, fluffy, curly hair would look wrong.

8. What style is most suitable to your age? Although your basic face shape does not change as you get older, your face does lose some of its fullness and become less smooth skinned. But don't be alarmed: gentle lines and creases really do add character and can create a distinctive and interesting look. Your hairstyle should allow for this: it should not compete with your face but should flatter it. Too many curls and frills or hair that is too long or full would be in definite competition with your face. An easy, soft, natural hairstyle is best for older women.

What are the best bets for the general body types?

The *Renoir* (and all generously proportioned women) usually looks good with a feminine, soft hairdo—curly, wispy, and romantic. The style could be as complicated as a modified Gibson Girl or as simple as a slightly curled shag, but there should be a fullness, softness, and slight roundness. An Audrey Hepburn gamine cut would be completely wrong. Can you picture Elizabeth Taylor in a gamine cut?

The *Athlete* usually looks good in short, boyish hair, especially a short, layered haircut, a little longer at the nape of the neck. A full-bodied look would be good, but no frills or curls.

The *Pear* generally looks good in short, feminine hairstyles with some fullness. Chin-length hair is always flattering and should adjust its shape to the shape of the face.

The *Bulge* (or one that's angular, without the bulge) can wear her hair a little longer than shoulder length. Soft, full, layered hair looks feminine and sexy. But if the hair is *too* full, it can overwhelm.

The *Clothes Rack* (and anybody who

tends to be long and lanky) usually has to wear her hair somewhat long or her head will look out of proportion with the rest of her body.

GENERAL TIPS AND HINTS. Today's look is natural—your hair should move. It should also fit in comfortably with your life-style. If you have to spend more than 30 minutes on it each morning, consider a new cut.

If, like the majority of women in America, you have experimented with some form of hair coloring or plan to do so in the future, keep in mind that it is not wise to stray too far from your natural color aura. A 180-degree turnabout tends to look contrived and will require a partial, if not complete, restructuring of your wardrobe.

Consider your hair within the context of your outfit. It may be advisable to vary your basic hairstyle, depending on the mood and proportions of your clothes. A hairstyle that makes the head appear smaller would be suitable to the proportions of a jacket with padded shoulders and a tapered waist, for example; whereas a long evening dress may call for a fuller hairstyle. A silk blouse with a mandarin collar might look attractive with hair that is pulled gently back on the sides, whereas a boat-neck cotton shirt is very compatible with a loose, free style that falls to the shoulders.

Experiment with decorative combs, barrettes, and other hair accessories, and discover the various looks you can achieve without actually changing your basic cut. If you experiment in front of your full-length mirror, it will be easy to see the subtle proportional shifts the variations allow.

Shoulder-length hair allows for many hairstyle options. Here are six examples, from a loose free look to an elegant chignon.

There are many hairstyling techniques that can produce a new look just for a day, allowing you to be adventurous without taking on the longer term commitment of a new cut or permanent. The following are just a sampling, but if you begin to enjoy switching hairdos on occasion, check through some of the many hairstyling magazines for new ideas.

To fix your hair in *rolls*, section the hair in pielike sections, pull each section together as if you were going to make a ponytail and twist it, tuck in the ends and secure them with hairpins. It won't look twisted but rather will have a rolled look. You can do this with medium- or long-length hair but not with hair that's very short.

If you want a *frizzy look* for one day only, section your hair into the same pielike divisions, twist each one until you can't twist it any more, and put it on the smallest roller you can find, or a permanent wave rod. Leave your hair this way for an hour. When you take the rollers out, it will be frizzy. Because of its increased bulk, your hair will also have a better texture for creating the rolled hairstyles.

If your hair isn't very long and you want a slightly different look, take a section of hair above each ear, twist it until it forms a narrow coil, draw the coil toward the back and top of your head, and secure it with a comb, hairpin, or barrette. The coiled hair will resemble a narrow, braided hair band.

If you want to set your hair in hot rollers, but want to get away from the full, pouffy look and make your hairstyle a little more contemporary, twist the hair about four times before you put it on the roller. It keeps the hair from getting too full on top and pushes the fullness to the bottom.

If your hair is not in great condition, hot rollers can further damage it. An alternative is to twist dry hair, roll it in perm rods, then get in the shower and let the steam set it for you (take care not to get your hair wet).

As the fashion silhouettes become smaller and narrower, the head will get smaller. Both Suga and Martin feel that short hair—a small head—will be with us for a while. A small head refers to hairstyles in which the hair is kept close to the skull—either cut short or worn up. The classic ponytail, gathered at the nape of the neck, will produce this effect, as will a pair of braids crossed over in front or back and wrapped around the head, or long hair swept up and pinned in a twist or chignon. If you wear your hair down, the fullness should be farther down and not at the scalp. More Rita Hayworth than Farrah Fawcett.

If you keep your hair in good condition, it can be a very beautiful, natural ornament.

MAKEUP

Cosmetics, like any other accessory, can add a real spark to your basic look: a little blush can bring a healthy glow to your cheeks, a bit of lipstick or colored gloss can give your lips a dash of color, and the wave of a mascara wand can make your eyes look bigger and brighter. The trick is to keep your makeup looking light and natural while it works its wonders for you. The over-made-up face is a thing of the past—throw out your pancake makeup. Models that I grew up with in the business look fresher and spunkier today than they did when we first started, thanks to the natural makeup trend.

People who have style generally have a strong self-image and positive self-esteem—a strong sense of being.
WAY BANDY

Makeup application is a real skill for which you need a thorough understanding of your face—its contours, bone structure, and basic shape—and of your equipment—the cosmetics, brushes, puffs, as well as the techniques and tricks of application. I recommend Way Bandy's book *Designing Your Face.* He explains all the "do's" in detail and provides warnings about the common pitfalls.

Until you have time to study and practice the art of cosmetics, a good thing to keep in mind is that, as with jewelry, *less is more.* Don't overdo it. If you are looking slightly pale, perk up your face with a light application of blush. If you wear a foundation, make sure there's no line of demarcation and that it matches your skin tone. The essential point is to look natural, while subtlely playing up the

For daytime, keep your makeup light and natural.

best features of your face. And that's the other important thing to remember: it's *your* face. With cosmetics, just as with clothes, you have to develop your own style. Your face—skin tone, skin qualities, bone structure—is unique. It would be disastrous to try to imitate verbatim the makeup that looks perfect on someone else.

Sunny Griffen told me that when she first started modeling, she tried to copy the makeup techniques of some of her idols within the profession:

> It never worked. It was the days of pancake, and I put that on and I looked like a little street urchin. It just never worked. What finally happened was *Bazaar* got hold of me, an editor washed off all the terrible makeup that I was wearing to look like other people, put a fan on my hair, and all of a sudden there was my career—I had the natural look. The whole industry started to change about that time, from the "perfect-feature era" to the sort of imperfect, windblown, natural look.

The look of today has evolved from that.

Your style is your total being, from the way you walk to the way you apply your cosmetics to your choice of clothes. Don't imitate; be your own person, and use your cosmetics to help you attain that goal. With makeup, as well as with hair, jewelry, scarves, and other accessories, it is important to find an approach that expresses you. By all means experiment, but only borrow what you can adapt to yourself without compromising *your* look.

FASHION SMARTS

RECYCLING, NEW IDEAS FOR MOTHERS-TO-BE, AND QUALITY CLOTHES

Most likely there are items already in your closet that can be updated—belted, unbelted, altered, accessorized, and generally renovated—and made to suit the person you want to be this year. Many other pieces in your closet can go directly to the Salvation Army as a charitable donation, offering an added bonus of a tax deduction. The decision about what to rejuvenate for this year, store for possible future use, or banish from your sight forever, should be based on *quality*. There is no reason to try to update a $5.98 polyester button-down shirt. This type of garment can safely be classified as a throwaway. On the other hand, the recycling of a seasoned pair of leather pants, a time-honored cashmere sweater, or a treasured antique fur coat may certainly prove to be worth the bother. This is a very good reason why you should buy quality in the first place.

BUY THE BEST—JUST BUY LESS

A new fashion look is usually a mere shift in line and/or proportion, a change in the basic silhouette, from loose and roomy to neat and streamlined, from a boxy to a tapered shape, from flare-leg to narrow-leg pants, or from wide to narrow collars or lapels. Fortunately, classic, fine-quality fabrics are as integral a part of any new fashion look as they are of an old one, thereby allowing us to integrate some of our "oldies but goodies" into our current wardrobe.

Basic well-cut shirts and skirts can look current and fashionable for years with a few new accessories and a casual roll of the sleeve.

The fashion silhouette of today is neat and trim. But because fashion is presently so individual, the real fashion silhouette today is your body. Since the conception of this book, the "in" fashion silhouette has gone from very unconstructed, roomy, boxy, and loose to slim and narrow. While I was quite aware of this line modification, I did not make a drastic change in my style; but I did alter my line slightly, almost unconsciously. My body shape was still my body shape, and there were still proportional best bets for it. So I adapted the new line to the old line and spent very little money and energy doing it. I bought one or two new pair of trousers and tucked in some of last season's "big tops." Effortless. This is why I stress flexibility, imagination, and individuality.

REJUVENATING YOUR CLOTHES

Everything can be altered, nothing is so sacred that it cannot be changed. This is my basic fashion precept. I have noticed that people are often very reluctant to remodel an expensive piece of clothing, especially when it has a famous designer label tacked in back. Rather than alter the garment, it seems they prefer to leave this piece of art hanging in its sanctuary, untouched by human hands, even though they will not wear it in its present state. This is a huge waste. Adjust it, remake it, renovate it, wear it. Clothes are made to be worn, not idolized.

Another bit of advice on this same subject: *do not save all your best clothes for a special occasion.* You should wear your favorites every day. If you save them too long, they'll be outmoded anyway. Treat yourself well; wear your best and feel good. Don't worry about ruining anything by wearing it too much. Clothing is only important if you're enjoying it, and wearing it is the way to enjoy it.

Jackets

Jacket styles are actually quite easy to alter. It is usually the lapel width and shape that dates a jacket. You would be surprised how a one-half to three-fourths of an inch shift in the lapels will make a major change in the total look of a jacket. At present, lapels are narrow. Slimming down wide lapels is a simple operation. Look through a few fashion magazines. Pick the lapel line you like, and ask your neighborhood tailor to try to duplicate it. If lapels should happen to get wider again someday, you'll just have to worry about that later. But lapel variations are one of the slowest movers in fashion, so you have time.

Remember your proportions. Your jackets might be a bit too short or too long. Again, length is an individual consideration. The right length is the length that is most flattering to you.

To determine *your* jacket length, put on an outfit you intend to wear with the jacket. Stand in front of your irreplaceable full-length mirror. Put on the jacket and pin it up one-half inch or so with a few straight pins. You will see the proportions change. Pick the length you like, and alter the jacket accordingly. And don't worry about shoulder pads; they can easily be added or subtracted.

Sleeve length is a factor that I very seldom worry about. I usually fold my shirt sleeve over the jacket sleeve, give it a roll, and follow

Perk up last year's sweater with a belt and some innovative jewelry.

with a casual push. If the sleeve is a little too long or short, so what? It gives me the comfortable, relaxed look that has become my style. Fashion experts used to say that the correct sleeve length was just long enough to cover the top of the wristbone, letting the shirt sleeve peek out a quarter of an inch. That still works.

You can wear any kind of pin on a jacket for a little extra interest. Even a small tea rose is good for a dash of color and a wonderful scent. Wear your collars up or down. Wear your scarves over or under. Play around. See how you feel the most comfortable—what you choose may simply depend on what the day holds for you. You can give the impression of being young and spirited or mature and dependable—whatever you like—by the way you wear your clothes.

Shirts

Don't forget your closet. You may come across some great finds. For instance, if you like everything about a shirt but have stopped wearing it because of its outmoded collar, get rid of it—the collar, that is. Hold on to the shirt. Removing a collar is very easy. It won't cost you more than five dollars at your tailor's, probably less. The no-collar look is very compatible with average or short necks.

Another home or close-to-home shopping tip? Don't overlook the men in your life; they may have some shirts that they are bored with. If the color suits you and the shirt is made of quality fabric, take the collar off and you have a new-look baggy shirt. Tuck it in. Belt it. Tie it at the waist. Wear it over T-shirts, other shirts, camisoles, bathing suits. If it's too long, cut off the bottom and hem it.

My ex-boyfriend used to get a lot of reject shirts from his lawyer, a rather dapper dresser with buying fever. Every couple of months when there was a lull in his law practice, he would run out, buy some new shirts, and give us his expensive, hardly worn, monogrammed shirts from the last lull. After having the monograms removed, my friend had himself several nice new shirts. I would leave the monograms on and remove the collars. Inevitably, someone would ask me what the initials stood for, and I'd tell them "my boyfriend's lawyer in New Jersey." "Oh," they would reply.

Old shirts can always be worn under sweaters or other shirts for a splash of color at the neck or cuffs. You don't have to be traditional and wear a crew-neck sweater with your shirt collar out (still one of my favorite outfits when I want to look eighteen). A mandarin

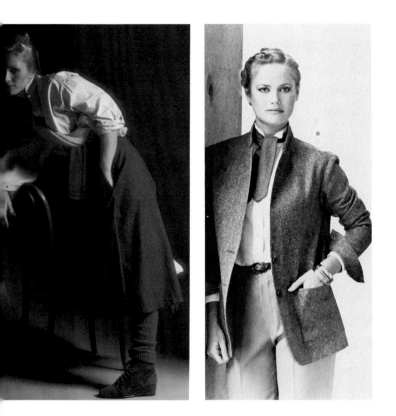

It's the way you wear old clothes that gives them new zest. Push up your sleeves, tie a sweater over your shoulders, turn up your collar, and introduce an unusual accessory—even a boy's tie will do.

"no-collar" look works well under a crew neck as well.

T-shirts that are too large can be knotted on the bottom. Shirt sleeves of *any* style can be rolled up to *any* length. Slip a vest over an old shirt, if you're so inclined, or an old shirt over a new camisole.

Remember all the various things you can do with shirts to make them fit you. If you happen to spot a terrific flannel or wool shirt in an army-navy or sporting-goods store, don't rule it out.

Sweaters

Sweaters, although difficult to alter (pull the wrong piece of wool and turn the sweater right over to your daughter or your niece), can be maneuvered to achieve the current look. Thin-to medium-bulk sweaters can be stylishly tucked into a loose-fitting pair of pants. This looks great worn under a wool or flannel shirt. (Remember the one you loved in the army-navy store?) If it's a bit snug with both the sweater and the shirt tucked in, tie the shirt at the waist—over the belt—or above the waistline, or below, depending on what looks the best on you.

You can casually flip a sweater over your shoulders and tie it, or tuck the sleeve ends into the top of your pants (like suspenders). Try shirts with different collars under sweaters. Experiment with styles that you might not have thought would work. And if you still have sweaters you don't think work this year, put them on hold and try them again next year.

PREGNANCY CAN GIVE BIRTH TO NEW IDEAS FOR OLD CLOTHES

Pregnancy is one of the best times to make use of your friendly old clothes. There is absolutely no reason to rush out and buy any of those insipid little-mother dresses the minute you get the high sign from your doctor. Many of the clothes designed especially for pregnant women are awful, although I've recently noticed some improvement. It is almost as if they're trying to program us into being perfect Gerber mothers.

I first became aware of these offensive designs when I had to pull together a wardrobe for a Johnson's Baby Powder commercial. It was impossible to find anything attractive and, in addition, I was locked into a particular color scheme that made my task doubly difficult (the clothes had to blend well with the wallpaper of the set bedroom). I finally ended up making the dress myself. And since I never have been one to look for extra work, you know it was an emergency.

Which clothes that you probably have in your closets are suitable for pregnancy?

1. All your full, roomy, blousey, tunic-type tops.

2. Your husband's old sweaters and shirts.

3. Drawstring pants. (This includes sweat pants, which are conducive to staying in shape during your pregnancy.)

4. Caftans and any of your "tent" dresses.

5. Skirts or slacks with elastic waists. (Any of your long elastic-top skirts can be pulled up above your breasts for a cool, loose cover-up in summer.)

6. Men's jogging shorts.

If you feel you need to buy a few new items, go into your local boutiques and department stores before the maternity shops. In the lingerie departments you can generally find elegant caftans and pajama pants with elastic waists that, worn with a loose tunic top, can work wonderfully as evening wear. Indian specialty shops frequently have colorful tunic tops. Mexican shops always have loose, waistless dresses that are perfect for the expectant mother. Buy your sweaters in the men's de-

A large man's sweater worn over an old skirt with an elastic waistband or your favorite tent dress—a few of the fashions for pregnancy that you may already own.

partments, and while you are there browse quickly through the shirts; the perfect tunic top might be there waiting for you. Lightweight rain slickers, available in sporting-goods and boat-supply stores, will keep you dry; cashmere shawls will keep you warm and cuddly; and embroidered shawls will protect you from drafts.

The main point I want to make is that there are many alternatives to boring clothes found in maternity departments. It is still possible to be in style while you're pregnant. It just takes a little imagination.

Stay away from the deadly pink-flowered, cap-sleeved, bowed-under-the-bust look—save this mood for your shower caps. Even before you decide to have the little tyke, while he's still a mere twinkle in your eye, as you meander through your favorite stores check out the kinds of things that might work for you when you're with child. That way, when the day comes, you will be ready.

Oh, one last word here. Beverly Johnson told me the only real investment she made while she was pregnant was in shoes. High heels are unhealthful and uncomfortable while carrying extra weight. She wore either low cowboy boots or sandals. Whatever style you opt for, keep the heels sensibly low. And, by the way, congratulations.

QUALITY CLOTHES

This book wouldn't be complete without my giving you some standards for recognizing clothing that is well made. It is not only a matter of cost, for high-priced dresses can occasionally contain as many substandard features as the weekly specials in the bargain basement.

Whether a garment is expensive or not, there are some tip-offs for determining its quality. Here are a few things to be aware of:

1. Good-quality fabric.

2. Well-finished seams (no puckering).

3. The inside should be well finished (no hanging threads, sloppy workmanship).

4. Buttons should be mother-of-pearl, wood, or bone (not plastic).

5. The zipper should be put in straight and should meet evenly and be covered by a flap of cloth.

6. Hems should be straight and finished properly. You should not see the stitching of the hemline or puckering on the outside of a skirt or dress.

7. If there is a slit in the dress, one side should not be longer than the other.

8. Collars should fall without buckling.

9. Cotton flannel shirts should be woven, not printed (if the inside of the shirt doesn't look the same as the outside, it is printed).

These tips should help you filter out poorly made clothes. They also pertain to antique clothes. But even if these old-timers are well made, it is often a good idea to have their seams reinforced by a tailor or seamstress as a preventive measure. The years can leave a subtle mark. This is just one more strategy that contributes to what I mean by "fashion smarts."

Now let's examine style, the most sophisticated of the fashion factors. You're ready for it.

STYLE

AND THE PERSONALITY FACTOR

So many varying ingredients go into making up one's personal style that an actual definition of this amalgam is all but impossible. But there is no doubt that style is shaped more by the subjective factors of attitude and personality than by the concrete principles of fashion. Proportion, line, color, and texture are merely the tools of style. Willi Smith puts it quite well:

> Style is the person—a person who believes in herself so much and is so aware of the way *she* wants to look that she just puts it over. When you see people who have a *personal* conviction about the way they want to look, they look great. They can be wearing something from the 20s, something from the 70s; it doesn't matter. Style comes from within and is simply displayed on the exterior.

In December 1975, Diana Vreeland organized an exhibition at the Costume Institute of the Metropolitan Museum of Art called American Women of Style. Stella Blum's written introduction to the exhibit explained the significance of the show and of the women it celebrated (including such monuments of fashion as Elsie de Wolfe; Mrs. Charles Dana Gibson; Consuelo, Duchess of Marlborough; Mrs. John W. Garrett; Gertrude Vanderbilt Whitney; Isadora Duncan; Rita de Acosta Lydig; Irene Castle; Millicent Rogers; and Josephine Baker):

> The clothes they wore were not so much a matter of joining the ranks of the fashionable but a manifestation of their own individuality. Often they came up with their own designs or put together unusual combinations. . . . Even when they wore the designs of others, they still managed to give the impression that their clothes were made only for them. . . . They reached beyond their times, as well as into other peri-

ods and places to develop a style that is essentially American in spirit and completely a projection of themselves.

The key words used to describe these women throughout the exhibition are the key words of style itself: energetic, determined, good humored, graceful, charming, witty, humble, vital, colorful, adventurous, dedicated, involved, effervescent, and kind.

When you stop and think of some of the men and women whose names are synonymous with style, it is easy to see that it's more than their clothes; it is their personalities, their carriage, their attitude, their movements and manner of speech that are memorable (for example, Greta Garbo, Marlene Dietrich, Grace Kelly, Lauren Bacall, Katharine Hepburn, Humphrey Bogart, Clark Gable, Fred Astaire, Gary Cooper, John F. Kennedy). Their dress, while a delightful embellishment, allowed their personalities to shine through. And that's the real trick to style. As Perry Ellis notes, "Clothes constantly reflect what a person's about, but they don't alter or change it. They might alter the image of what that person thinks she's about, but it's the substance, the continuity of the person that's important."

While you can't adopt someone else's style, you can learn from those whose style you admire by simply observing and understanding why their clothes work for them. Only then can you adapt a few of their princi-

Marlene Dietrich, a woman who is the
very embodiment of individual style.

I try to design my clothes to allow a woman's own style or personality to come through. They should have the freedom to add jewelry, feathers, or go unadorned—the freedom to do their own personal thing.
JOAN SIBLEY

ples to fit your individual criteria. I agree with Calvin Klein:

> There's no point in trying to look like an editorial out of *Vogue* every month. That's not the way to do it. The way to develop style is to try to develop a certain look of your own, something of *you* that people can identify you with, and to be adaptable to change. But just to try to look like a page out of a magazine is silly. If you do, you become a victim of fashion.

FINDING YOUR STYLE

Don't force the issue of style. Your style will develop gradually as you practice the basics of fashion we've discussed and become increasingly aware of the importance of your individuality. As your confidence builds in your knowledge of proportion, line, color, texture, and accessories, you'll find yourself taking more chances, having more fun, and your style will emerge. Meanwhile, keep these basics in mind:

1. *Wear your clothes; don't let them wear you.* You want to be remembered for who you are, not for your red polka-dot dress.

2. *Keep it simple.* If you do decide to go all out and call a lot of attention to yourself, make sure you can handle the reactions. I always have to chuckle when I hear a woman in a transparent blouse or an outlandishly tight

The pure lines of this black dress create a spare and elegant image. Simplicity is the key to chic.

*A more flashy statement. This style is
bound to get a reaction.*

shirt, dress, or pair of pants complaining about the stares she's getting. I mean, really, who's not going to look?

3. *Subtlely play up your strengths.* Your best quality can be any part of the total you: skin, hair, intelligence, the timbre of your voice. Figure out what you like best about yourself and let it shine like a beacon.

It's interesting to note that in *The Great Gatsby*, Fitzgerald attributes Daisy Buchanan's mystery and charm more to her voice than to her physical appearance. In the words of Nick Carraway, his narrator:

> I looked back at my cousin, who began to ask me questions in her low thrilling voice. It was the kind of voice that the ear follows up and down, as if each speech is an arrangement of notes that will never be played again. . . . There was an excitement in her voice that men who had cared for her found difficult to forget: a singing compulsion, a whispered "listen," a promise that she had done gay, exciting things just a while since and there were gay, exciting things hovering in the next hour.

4. *Don't try to alter your style or personality to suit the occasion.* Don't try to be the kind of person you think "they" would like. Obvious as this may sound, it's a trap that ensnares a great many people, perhaps because we've all been programmed for acceptance since early childhood. This way of thinking isn't relevant to life today, when individuality is prized and respected.

Feeling natural and unself-conscious is an earmark of great style, and it shows in the way you carry your clothes. While it's a cinch to be free and easy in a casual situation with close friends, it's more of a challenge when you find yourself in more formal surroundings. People have a tendency to stiffen up the second they see "black tie" engraved on an invitation.

Style is comfort and a fearless confidence.
BETHANN HARDISON

There's simply no reason to become tense or self-conscious in these "rarefied" social situations. Just be you. It's positively refreshing to meet a "real" person at some stuffy event. Be yourself at all times. That's style!

5. *Stick with the colors, lines, and shapes that work for you.* If every time you wear a certain shade of blue, for instance, you get twenty-two comments on how great you look and how beautiful your eyes are, why go looking for a green blouse? Stick with the winners. And the same goes for a neckline or a cut of slacks. By all means, experiment—but remember you always have the winners to come back to.

Self-awareness is an obvious prerequisite to true style. But it is important that once you know your body and your personality and once you have put the fashion principles that we have discussed to practical application, you begin to trust *your* instincts. Wear what you now *know* will make you feel comfortable and look good.

It might interest you to learn that even those of us in the fashion world make mistakes now and then—no one will deny this. When you begin experimenting, you will probably make a few mistakes. So what? Mistakes are an inevitable part of any growth process. But if you proceed slowly, trying new colors, lines, and styles one at a time, the mistakes will be minimal and less costly.

Why not use this book to help you to organize your fashion lessons? First study the ideas in a chapter, then put them into practice. Once you have mastered one chapter, move on to the next. As with learning to ride a bicycle, swim, or perform any skill, once you understand the concept and learn how to execute it, it is with you for the rest of your life.

But be prepared: it sometimes takes years to arrive at a style that you can be comfortable with. Dressing uniquely requires time to develop and perfect. Do not be disappointed if your success is not immediately apparent.

Attitude, mannerisms, and personality are all important elements of fashion that determine how our clothing looks.

Mental comfort is a key consideration when settling on a personal style. This woman probably wouldn't feel dressed without her hat and white gloves.

Irish face and the freckles. I wanted a whole new look for myself. I was single again and wanted to make a change. So I had my hair straightened and dyed black and wore it pulled back slick. I affected bull-fighter hats and ruffled blouses cut to the navel, a long cigarette holder, and I put a mole on the side of my face with dark eye shadow. I had fun with it at first. Men looked at me in a much different way than they did when I had my red hair and freckles. But one night, as I was getting ready to go out I got a glimpse of myself in the mirror and I started to giggle. I practically fell on the floor laughing. I thought, "What are you doing, I mean, this is crazy." And once you start to laugh, of course, the whole thing falls apart. I couldn't carry it off any more. But it was a great exercise and got me over the fear of trying something new.

I don't suggest any change quite as abrupt as Nina's. But it does go to show that change can be fun, and should certainly not be intimidating. Experiment until you find your style, using your new fashion savvy as a guide. I guarantee that any time and effort invested will pay off in the comfort and fun you will have dressing in *your* own style.

Nina Blanchard related an amusing anecdote. Before she had her own agency she held seminars on how to get into television and movies. In one class she wanted to prove that within reasonable boundaries you can be anything you want to be. They were discussing certain classic types—the girl next door, the femme fatale, the shrinking violet—and how these stereotypes were cast for motion pictures. She tried an experiment:

I've always wanted to be dark and seductive and Spanish looking. And here I am with the

I think that people are too interested in what other people are wearing. The sense of competition is totally demoralizing. You've got to think of yourself and not how everyone else is dressed.
DIANA VREELAND

I don't like clothes that just cover the body. I like them to be another element in one's life, to be exciting.
JOAN SIBLEY

PLANNING IT ALL

CLOTHES TO FIT YOUR LIFE-STYLE

With all this information and 57 varieties of tips, hints, and options in your possession, I have no doubt that you are well on your way to accumulating and enjoying an inventive and practical wardrobe. Before I leave you to your own devices, however, I would like to offer a few final reminders, suggestions, and ideas on how to pull together some easy and original looks for your varied activities. All of them can be adapted to your personal taste and life-style.

The reminders

1. It is no longer mandatory to change your entire outfit every day. So buy the best and buy less. You are much better off wearing a few quality garments than a slew of mediocre ones. Apollonia agrees. "If I find something I really like, I could wear it for a week and feel totally comfortable. Even if the same people see me in it for a week, I feel brand new because I love it. I don't buy as many clothes as I used to."

2. It is easier to plan your wardrobe around pieces that will mix and match. But remember, things don't have to match exactly; they simply have to coordinate, or harmonize.

3. If you want to be able to put something on in the morning and forget about it for the rest of the day, buy clothing that fits well and styles that don't require constant fussing and readjusting.

These versatile silk dresses with simple lines will take you almost anywhere. They're a good investment for daytime and evening wear.

4. Because accessories can change an outfit's look, if you have a limited budget, buy simple, classic designs that can be easily dressed up or down with accessories.

5. Dressing should not be an attempt to break the four-minute mile. No one knows how much time you spend in front of your mirror. They only see the end result. Take your time and work on an outfit until it looks right. Even those who are most savvy about fashion do not arrive at the perfect look without some concentrated effort.

Because I believe most of us have different clothing needs for the different areas of our lives, I have provided three general wardrobe schemes, which should take you through your varied activities. Basically, we can divide our wardrobe requirements into these categories: daytime or work, evening, and leisure. Though the categories sometimes overlap, each has its own specific considerations. I will offer more detailed information about coat wardrobes and dressing for special occasions in separate sections, as these clothing needs deserve some special attention.

THE WORKING HOURS

Where you work and what you do—your job—is, of course, the deciding factor in shaping your working-hours' wardrobe.

CORPORATE IMAGE. I frankly don't subscribe to the philosophy of strictly defined dress codes for lawyers, executives, bankers, accountants. Men in these positions have no choice in the way they dress; they are bound by the convention that dictates very conservative suits. Although it is "permissible" to wear a brighter shirt or a more interesting tie now and then, anything other than a suit, even a conser-

You don't want to look bizarre in an office, but on the other hand, you want to have some individuality.
BILL BLASS

vative tweed sport jacket, is frowned upon. Women, on the other hand, have a few options, all of which fall within the bounds of propriety.

There are, needless to say, unspoken dress codes in every business. But if you are smart enough to be in a responsible position in the first place, you are smart enough to understand these unspoken codes and work within them. As I've said before, fashion should make your life easier; it should work for you, not against you.

Since it is obviously easier to do a good job with the respect and support of co-workers and clients—and the clothes you wear *are* an important part of the first impressions you make—the more responsible and competent you appear, the more initial respect you will get. Wearing clothes that flaunt your sexuality does not make any sense. This would, in effect, be challenging men to treat you as a sex object. Or, by wearing outrageous, bizarre outfits, you may be denying yourself the opportunity to be thought of as a serious and qualified businesswoman. Why fight city hall? You can still look individual and chic without looking like a Brazilian bombshell. So let's take a look at some of the options suitable for a corporate image and consider the one that would work best with your body type.

A tailored suit, of classic design, is a good investment for those who work in a traditional office environment. The blue pin-striped fabric makes this one especially neat and trim.

133

The suited look

This is the classic tailored look that is widely hailed as the proper image for the corporate career woman. With proper attention paid to detail it can be a very elegant look.

The advantages of this type of dress are its practicality, "travel ability," and versatility (it is ideal for mixing and matching). Here is what might be in such a wardrobe:

□ One three-piece suit (skirt, jacket, and vest) in a fabric and color such as gray flannel, navy wool, or a nubby brown tweed that will blend with the rest of your wardrobe.

□ One silk blouse in a solid color (beige, white, burgundy, or pale blue—a tone that is flattering to the color of your suit and your skin) or in a very small print pattern (with light gray, white, burgundy, or navy background).

□ Two cotton blouses: one with subtle stripes, one in a solid color (red, bright blue, rust).

□ Three sweaters: one good-quality turtleneck (oyster white); one V-neck cardigan sweater (cream color); one smartly styled pullover sweater (taupe).

□ Two extra skirts in navy, brown, or black flannel.

□ Two pairs of shoes: one spectator pump in deep brown or taupe; one high-heeled loafer in burgundy.

□ One handbag in burgundy leather.

□ A few minor accessories, including some scarves and belts, a tie, inexpensive costume jewelry for accent (a pin, a pair of earrings).

□ An overcoat, raincoat, and boots, if you live in a cold or rainy climate.

With these things, which are relatively few in number, you have the essential elements of a good-looking, practical, comfortable fall and winter wardrobe, as well as a whole collection of different looks. The same principle can easily be applied to a summer wardrobe by translating these winter fabrics into lightweight cottons, linens, and other summer fabrics.

BODY-TYPE CONSIDERATIONS. Because of its straight, nonfluid lines, an ultratailored suit would be most compatible with the more angular body types: the Clothes Rack, the Athlete, and the Bulge. It would not be best for the Renoir, unless the pieces conform to her silhouette. All the good points of this body type—its feminine curves, small waist, and graceful

roundness, would be camouflaged by the linear design of most ultratailored looks. A boxy, double-breasted jacket would be the worst choice.

The Pear could wear parts of this tailored look very successfully. A jacket with padded shoulders would help create a balance between her narrow top and broad bottom, and most skirts would be flattering to her. A vest worn open would create a good line, but worn closed and fitted it would hug the narrow torso and therefore emphasize her broad hips.

If you are a petite woman, you would do

With a gray three-piece suit as a basis, there is a range of possibilities for different looks. The skirt can be paired with a variety of blouses and sweaters, and worn with or without the jacket and vest.

A lightweight suit and matching blouse with soft, untailored lines are a neat and feminine look for a summer working wardrobe.

best to avoid classically tailored suits, especially the three-piece variety. Besides the inevitable problem of finding a good fit, the basic construction and stiffness of a classically tailored suit will make you appear even smaller than you are. Clothes with a softer, more fluid feeling are better for you.

COST CONSIDERATIONS. Wardrobes based on the three-piece tailored suit can vary greatly in price, and these costs will clearly differ depending on where you live. The selection of clothing previously listed can be bought for approximately $600 (without an overcoat, raincoat, and pair of boots). In addition, I have included some suggestions, and prices for wardrobe supplements, listed in order of priority. If you are able to afford a more generous wardrobe but still must maintain some restraint, a good assortment of suited-look clothing—again, without coats and boots—can cost you $1,200 and up. With the addition of an overcoat, raincoat, and boots, the suited-look wardrobes outlined in this section will come to anywhere from $1,000 to $1,700, plus tax.

If, like most of us, you are budget conscious, it's a good idea to buy the essentials first and add to them as the money becomes available, especially when you spot a good bargain. It is possible to buy good clothes for less money: it just takes more effort. Always keep your eyes open for end-of-season sales and shop the stores that specialize in discounting designer clothes. If you buy well-made, classic designs in fine-quality fabrics, you will be able to wear them for many years, updating your wardrobe with a few new blouses and accessories. I've outlined a general cost scheme here that ranges from a conservative approach to a freer and more generous clothing budget. As noted, prices will vary in different parts of the country, so you may not be able to find some of the items at the exact costs in this scheme.

THE SUITED - LOOK WARDROBE

Budget-Conscious

1 3-piece suit	$120
1 silk blouse	40
2 cotton blouses	50
2 sweaters	70
2 skirts	100
2 pairs of shoes	110
1 handbag	50
Belts, scarves, and miscellaneous accessories	60
TOTAL	$600

Plus:

1 overcoat	$200
1 raincoat	120
1 pair of boots	80
	$400
TOTAL	$1000

Bountiful

2 suits ($200 each)	$ 400
3 silk blouses (2 at $40; 1 at $80)	160
2 fine cotton blouses ($35 each)	70
3 sweaters (2 at $35; a high-quality cashmere for $80)	150
2 skirts ($50 each)	100
1 pair of slacks	70
2 pair of shoes	110
1 handbag	60
Belts, scarves, and miscellaneous accessories	80
TOTAL	$1,200

Plus:

1 good wool overcoat	$220
1 well-tailored raincoat	180
1 pair of fine leather boots	100
	$500
TOTAL	$1,700

Supplements

1 silk blouse (bright solid color)	$ 40
1 pair of slacks (navy or gray)	65
1 2-piece suit	100
1 fine cotton blouse (print)	35
1 cashmere sweater (pale blue)	60
TOTAL	$300

The unsuited look

If your look is softer, if you are not the suit type, or if you just don't like ultratailored fashions, you can be quietly elegant, refined, and every bit as put together. All you need are the following:

☐ Three skirts with soft lines (in different flattering styles—perhaps with gatherings and pockets or gently pleated) in beige, gray, and black.

☐ Two silk blouses: a cream-color or white and a small print (with gray or pale blue background).

☐ Three "beltable" cardigans in beige, gray, and black or rust color.

☐ One vest in a beige tone, something soft, perhaps crocheted.

☐ One light tan Chanel-type, no-collar shirt jacket.

☐ One soft shirtwaist-style silk dress.

☐ Add a few accessories—a long, narrow, subtly printed scarf, some costume jewelry (a pair of earrings, thin gold chain, a narrow bracelet), two belts.

☐ Two pairs of shoes: a classic Chanel slingback in beige with black toe, a luggage-color pump.

☐ One handbag in a natural tan.

☐ An overcoat, raincoat, and boots.

BODY-TYPE CONSIDERATIONS. This look can be modified to be made flattering to every body type. Unlike the suited look, which has more defined lines and therefore allows for fewer proportional shifts, this style of dressing leaves the field wide open. It is based on three pieces, but the shape of each piece can be custom selected by you with your body type and its variables in mind. For instance, you can

There's a demoralizing influence in the availability of too many clothes. One could be bewildered by the opportunities. In other words, I think it's almost more difficult with more things.

DIANA   VREELAND

choose a skirt with sewn-down front pleats if you are a little hippy, one with gentle folds if you are tall and lithe, or with a neat, trim line if you are of average build. The third piece (or second in the case of the silk dress), whether it is a vest, cardigan, or Chanel-type jacket, can vary in length, width, and style in accordance with your proportions and your personal taste. Any one of these third or second pieces allows for a much greater degree of flexibility than

the jacket of a three-piece suit, and will also afford you the option of adding an extra texture.

COST CONSIDERATIONS. This wardrobe also offers budget flexibility, since it is not organized around a central costly purchase such as a three-piece suit, and you may be able to find some of its components—cardigan sweaters, a vest, jacket, or shirtwaist dress—for substantially less than the figures I have projected. Another advantage of this wardrobe is that

Here are ten different unsuited looks, based on one dress and a variety of skirts, blouses, sweaters and accessories. These outfits are casual yet refined in feeling and will allow for a great deal of flexibility while using only a few basic components. Although they are soft and untailored, each has a beautifully put together look.

The better you know yourself, the better dresser you'll be. The more you know your body, the more you know your limitations, if there are any; the more you know yourself, the more you know how much comfort you need and how much you can give up. You know the colors that are good for you and how they'll work for you when you're wearing them. You know what hairstyle is good for you, and won't be pushed around by a hairdresser. All this comes from knowing yourself, having confidence, and liking yourself.

WILLI SMITH

some of its elements—such as skirts and shoes—may be priced considerably lower than comparable elements in the suited-look wardrobe. The more constructed clothing and accessories are often costly because of the more detailed workmanship. However, you will need a few more pieces than you do for the suited-look, without the versatile three-piece suit.

The essential elements of a *budget-conscious unsuited-look wardrobe* can be put together for $700, if you already own an overcoat, raincoat, and boots. The added expense of these items will bring the cost up to $1,100. As always, the proper shopping strategy will reduce the cost.

I have again offered some general budget schemes for low- to high-cost wardrobes.

A solid-color wool dress with a challis scarf in a delicate print is an attractive alternative to a suit or skirt and sweater for daytime wear.

THE UNSUITED LOOK WARDROBE

Budget-Conscious

3	skirts	$120
2	silk blouses	80
3	cardigan sweaters	105
1	vest	30
1	shirt-jacket	60
1	shirtwaist dress	80
2	pairs of shoes	100
1	handbag	50
	Belt, scarves, and miscellaneous accessories	75
	TOTAL	$700

Plus:

1	overcoat	$200
1	raincoat	120
1	pair of boots	80
		$400
	TOTAL	$1,100

Supplements

1	silk blouse (bright solid color)	$40
1	fine cotton blouse (print or stripe)	35
1	fine-quality skirt (natural tan, brown, or rust)	60
1	cashmere sweater (white or black turtleneck)	80
1	pair of slacks (tan, soft looking)	70
1	2-piece wool knit dress (burgundy)	125
	TOTAL	$400

Bountiful

4	skirts (2 at $40; 2 at $60)	$200
3	silk blouses (2 at $40; 1 at $80)	160
2	cotton blouses ($35 each)	70
2	cardigan sweaters (1 at $35; 1 at $50)	85
1	cashmere turtleneck sweater	80
1	cowl-neck wool sweater	45
1	vest	50
1	good quality shirt-jacket	75
2	shirtwaist dresses ($80 each)	160
1	2-piece wool knit dress	125
2	pairs of shoes	100
1	handbag	60
	Belts, scarves, and miscellaneous accessories	90
	TOTAL	$1,300

Plus:

1	overcoat	$220
1	raincoat	180
1	pair of boots	100
		$500
	TOTAL	$1,800

141

The expensively elegant look

A third possibility is a wardrobe composed of about ten very well made silk dresses. While this type of working wardrobe doesn't lend itself to as many diversified combinations, it is a very effective, feminine, refined and opulent look. (The opulence is not illusory, as the initial investment will probably be substantial.) Since this is exactly how Sunny Griffen put together her working wardrobe, I'll let her describe it:

> Everything I buy has a definite look. I buy very good things. I don't buy trendy things. My corporate wardrobe basically consists of ten terrific dresses. I think nothing of spend-ing a thousand dollars for a single dress, but I wear it and wear it and wear it. I never grow tired of it. My friends see me in it seven hundred times and say, "There goes Sunny in her Chloë" (a Karl Lagerfeld design). But that's fine, because as I travel a lot and do a lot of television shows and personal appearances, I always want to be seen in something spectacular. So I have these ten dresses that I've collected over the years. When I go away on a trip, I'll take eight of them. I may only be going away for two days, but I never know which one I'm going to wear that day, although I know any one of them will be perfect. They are all pure silk, so I travel with an iron. When I check into a hotel, I iron my dresses while I

These expensively elegant *dresses would be suitable for work in many environments, but they are advisable only if budget is of little concern.*

watch the "Tonight Show"; then they're all ready to go in the morning. Depending on how I feel and how I look, I'll choose my dress. It really works for me.

BODY-TYPE CONSIDERATIONS. This working wardrobe is hypothetically right for all body types, since the style of the dresses you choose is presumably up to you. However, certain body variables make wearing dresses difficult. If, for example, you are extremely long waisted or short waisted, or have very narrow shoulders and broad hips, or broad shoulders and narrow hips, finding a dress that fits properly will be a near impossible task. This is another reason (besides their obvious versatility) that separates have gained such favor over the years. The closer you are to ideal or average proportions, the easier it is to wear dresses.

COST CONSIDERATIONS. This kind of wardrobe can cost anywhere from $500 to $5,000, depending on your choice of dresses. But because I feel that these garments must truly be expensively elegant if this look is to work well, I do not recommend it unless budget is of minimum concern. (You might, however, consider incorporating a few extra-special dresses into one of the other working-wardrobe schemes.)

The less-structured look
If you work in a more casual environment—in the arts or media, for example—or if your base is more home than office, you probably have few restrictions on what you choose to wear. Your clothing can be as inventive and unique as you like as long as it makes you feel comfortable and appear neat and responsible. Your workday wardrobe will be very much like your leisure wardrobe, which we will be discussing shortly. However, if you need some additional guidance, you can use the suggestions

I have offered for suited and unsuited looks as food for thought, and adapt them to fit your life-style. For instance, you can create a blend of workday and leisure wardrobes by substituting jeans or slacks for skirts, plaid shirts for solids, camisoles for turtlenecks, pretty cotton prints for subdued stripes, or flat loafers for Chanel sling-backs. You can afford to be more fanciful with your clothes. Try some of the new accessories in the stores or invent your own. You can mix some of the leisure and workday ideas—your range of choices is almost unlimited.

This kind of casual attire is appropriate to an informal work environment and easily passes from business to leisure hours.

THE EVENING HOURS

Your evening activities may run the gamut of roasting marshmallows over a campfire to a gala première, with a hundred and one possibilities in between. But since it is wardrobe "idea provokers" we are looking for, let us take a conventional nighttime activity, such as dinner and the theater, and examine a few apparent fashion approaches.

1. *Casually chic.* Try this easy-to-put-together monochromatic look that will take you anywhere. It will work especially well in off-white or black. Take a pair of comfortable loose-fitting slacks in a nubby raw silk; an overshirt in the same or a related fabric; a camisole or tube top (depending on just how dressy you want to look, anything from cotton to satin will work); a good-looking wrap belt (the color is optional, but something in lavender would be smashing with off-white, and anything from burgundy to tan or black would be nice with black); and any chic comfortable sandal. Then pin something fanciful on your lapel (a small flower or your favorite antique pin), pull up the collar, roll the sleeves and give them a gentle push, hang one of your small pouches on your shoulder, and you are all set. A comfortable, informal, yet fresh and trim, dressy look.

This kind of outfit goes exactly where *you* take it. If you wear very high strappy sandals, use a bit more makeup and hair with a beautiful ornamental comb—it can be positively elegant. If you wear your hair down and casual,

Evening is the time to dress up and be dramatic.

This look depends on first-rate design, fit, and fabric, and a sophisticated, effective use of color. A pair of silk slacks and jacket in black with burgundy accents, or in off-white with lavender accents, would be casually elegant for evening.

keep the accessories sporty, wear low tan sandals rather than high heels, you'll look casual, easy, and free. And incidentally, you've just got yourself a great travel outfit. I always take my black version on short winter jaunts to the Caribbean. It is ideal; I need no other evening attire. And with a couple of bikinis, a pair of jogging shorts, a Hawaiian shirt or two, and the clothes I travel in (usually a pair of jeans), I'm almost luggage free.

2. *Simply elegant.* If you're going out directly after work and won't have time to go home and change, you might wear a simple beige silk shirtwaist dress to work. Bring a

A pair of dressy strap sandals, a belt, and jewelry will transform this office look to a simply elegant *dress for evening.*

For an interestingly chic look, wrap an embroidered shawl over a loose silk blouse and ankle-length velvet skirt.

pair of dressy strap sandals, a belt, and some jewelry with you. Then put your hair up. You have succeeded in changing your look from tailored to dressy with a minimum amount of effort.

3. *Interestingly chic.* Just try an ankle-length lightweight velvet skirt, a loose drapey silk blouse, an eye-catching accessory, and a striking embroidered shawl.

THE LEISURE HOURS

For puttering around the house, cleaning, doing homework from your job, watering plants, snuggling up with a good book, watching the World Series, doing laundry, *comfort* is the key word. You want to be mobile, unen-

The leisure hours are the time to enjoy wearing some of your personal fashion favorites.

cumbered, ready to do a few deep-knee bends when the urge hits. (Might as well keep fit while taking care of menial chores.) This is the time to do away with all confining garments and undergarments.

Sunny Griffen has a strong view in favor of comfortable leisure duds:

> Let's talk about things that are not comfortable. Number one on my least-comfortable-thing-in-the-world-to-wear is a bra. Number two is panty hose. Number three is high heels. I detest these things from a comfort point of view. While during my business day I feel dressed and elegant wearing a bra, panty hose, and high heels, I cannot deal with them at home. At home I must be comfortable. I come home from work; take off my silk dress, high heels, and panty hose; and put on my track suit. I tie my hair back, remove my makeup, and that's how I live the rest of my life. If I stayed dressed, I couldn't be rough-and-tumble with my children, I couldn't work around the house, I couldn't cook in the kitchen (I'd always be afraid I'd splatter something on my silk dress).

At home we should be comfortably dressed, ready to spring into action and handle any and all eventualities. Here are a few leisure-look ideas:

Sweat shirts, sweat pants, and variations on the theme

These "classics" are my favorites, and a wardrobe *must* as far as I'm concerned. Why do I hold them in such high esteem?

1. The price is right. Approximately six dollars each in any army-navy store.

2. They last forever, launder like a dream, and require no ironing. The best are 100 percent cotton (check the label). The quality is superior to the synthetic blends, and they look better as they age. But get a size or two larger if you get all cotton, as it does shrink.

3. They come in great colors: red, bright yellow, navy, gray, light blue, forest green, white. Only shirts come in turquoise, black, and purple (pants in these colors may exist, but I haven't seen them, and I'm always on the lookout for a new addition to my collection).

4. They feel wonderful next to the skin; they're warm, cuddly, soft, incredibly comfortable, and absolutely unencumbering.

5. No underwear is necessary.

6. They are versatile. You can always wear a sweat shirt with jeans or corduroy slacks, or over a cashmere turtleneck, a plaid flannel shirt, or even a silk blouse. Believe it or not, a sweat shirt, slacks, and silk blouse can look very fashionable.

If the total sweat-shirt look is a bit too rough hewn for you, you can get the two-toned velour version. It has the same convenience and effect, but it's a bit more refined and expensive. Or, if you like the sweat-shirt idea but are not comfortable in pants, you might try a "monk's robe," which is a half-zippered front, ankle-length sweat shirt that's great for around the house, belted or unbelted. It is available at army-navy stores for about ten dollars.

For summer, simply trade in your sweat suit for oversized jogging shorts and an oversized man's V-necked undershirt. Comfort, comfort, comfort.

Slacks

A slightly more reserved look that is perfect for cold winter and fall days in the country is leather jeans (leather is incredibly warm—a classic), and a cashmere turtleneck that is topped with either a plaid wool overshirt or a man's V-necked sweater. Going outside? Take off the overshirt and put on a tweed blazer. Leather jeans also look great with a drapey silk shirt. The contrast in textures makes for an elegant yet informal look.

This leisure look, a classic for cold or rainy weather, will see you through many seasons' wear.

If leather is not your cup of tea, the same effect can be had with corduroy trousers. A friend of mine, Jane Hitchcock, found a great gray wool-flannel vest at an army-navy store for twelve dollars that she wears with her old corduroys, an antique plaid shirt, and riding boots. Comfortable—yet she looks like a fashion plate.

BODY-TYPE CONSIDERATIONS. Which body types should wear slacks and which ones should not? It is impossible to say. It is really a matter of individual comfort—both mental and physical. Some women are just not comfortable in slacks. But if you do want to wear them, there is such a huge variety of cuts and styles that you should be able to find a pair that is right for you—although granted it will be more difficult for some than others.

The two major problems that women usually experience with pant fit are (1) the length of the rise (the distance from the waist to the crotch—it is either too short or too long, and (2) the waist–hip ratio—if one area fits, the other does not. The only remedy for the rise-length problem is to keep shopping, and when you find a pair that fits properly, stay with that manufacturer. Although manufacturers and designers change pant-leg widths and other design details, they very often keep the same basic construction season after season (not unlike Detroit). If you really have a rough time finding a good fit, consider having slacks custommade.

The waist-hip problem can usually be remedied through minor alterations. Find slacks that fit well through the thighs and hips, and have the waist taken in by your local tailor. The Renoir and the Pear are likely to run across this problem more often than not.

If you have heavy hips or thighs, be sure to avoid slacks in very lightweight fabrics, such as matte jersey, silk, or cotton muslin, and by all means stay away from jeans. All the jeans from Calvin Klein, Gloria Vanderbilt, and various Italian and French designers look best on lanky bodies. You can get the casual jean feeling by wearing lightweight corduroy or medium-weight cotton slacks that are relatively loose around the hips and thighs. You might check out Willi Smith's slacks. His designs are usually very flattering on bodies that are not the classic model type, and they are also reasonably priced.

Dresses and skirts

As I said, slacks are not flattering for everyone, so let's consider dresses and skirts.

1. A loose, tunic-style dress that can be worn with turtlenecks or shirts underneath is one practical and fashionable alternative to pants. And you can always add a scarf for a little extra pizazz.

2. A comfortable skirt paired with a man's V-neck sweater always works.

3. Any soft, comfortable summer dress with an easy skirt is a potential candidate for your leisure hours and can easily be "winterized" with an oversweater or undersweater,

A simple summer dress can be worn all year round with warm sweaters, tights, and boots.

tights, and boots. Even a soft, feminine antique dress that you've only considered for specific occasions and climates can be adapted for more extended wear by adding a sweater and tights.

4. For hot summer days one of my favorite tricks is to take a long skirt with an elastic waist, pull it up over my bosom, and belt it loosely. Bingo! A cool strapless summer dress!

COATS

If you live in a four-season climate, your wardrobe should consist of three basic types of coats: one for every day that can pass gracefully from daytime to evening; one for winter leisure activities that can also serve as an emergency backup to your everyday coat in snowstorms and other extreme weather conditions; a classic trenchcoat, preferably with a removable lining, that can span the seasons.

Coats are another clothing essential where I do not advise compromise. Buy the best and you will be able to wear your coats season after season. Since these are major purchases and you will probably require more than one coat to meet the different needs of your life-style, it is especially important to choose your coats with care.

When you are selecting a coat, keep in mind the best bets and risks for your body type. Most of the general rules of proportion that apply to other areas of fashion apply to coats as well. A quick refresher:

☐ Shoulders: if they are narrow or sloping, consider a coat with shoulder pads. If you are broad shouldered, a style without defined shoulder seams would be a good bet.

☐ Waists: a style with a wide belt would be flattering to a long-waisted body. If you have a short waist, a coat without a defined waist, or

A coat with straight lines and padded shoulders will make narrow shoulders look broader. The fur scarf also helps give the impression of greater breadth.

the dimensions of your hips. If you have small hips, almost any style of coat will look work for you.

☐ Hemline: Your coat should be at least half an inch longer than your ideal hemline for skirts and dresses.

Here, then, is a closer look at the different kinds of coats you will need.

Your everyday coat—the working hours. Your everyday coat should be warm, practical, and good looking, and since it will be your constant companion for a good part of each year, it should ideally be one of your favorite garments. Your coat often helps you create your first impression, so be sure to select one that will make you feel comfortable when you wear it to the office or business appointments. A coat of relatively simple design in a subtle dark color that is flattering to your skin tone would be the best choice. A pale color

in a style that would permit the waistline to be lowered, would be best. A coat without a defined waist would also be ideal for anyone with a thick middle.

☐ Bust lines: if you have a generous bosom, avoid coats with bodice details. For a small-busted body, almost any style coat will do.

☐ Necks: a coat with a high collar would be most flattering to a long-necked body. If you have a short neck, consider a collar style that is designed to be worn low but that can be flipped up for windy days.

☐ Hips: if you have large hips, remember to make sure that the proportions of the top of the coat are not so narrow that they emphasize

The dark color, loose fit, and trim lines of these coats make them a best bet for women with thick waists or full hips.

With the addition of only a few smart accessories, your everyday coat can make an individual fashion statement.

would need to be cleaned too often and would not be as suitable for evening.

The fabric you choose for this coat and the other coats in your wardrobe is a matter of your taste, budget limitations, and need for protection against the cold.

There are many fine-quality wools available that will serve your purpose well. Most good wool coats have nice, trim lines and lack the bulky appearance of many fur coats and the currently popular nylon or cotton goose-down-filled parkas and coats. Cashmere is the ultimate wool coat. It is incredibly warm, has a wonderful soft feel, lasts forever, and always looks elegant. But it is expensive. If you do splurge on a cashmere coat, make sure it is of a classic design that is unlikely to become dated, so that you will be able to keep it until it simply becomes too worn to wear.

Nylon goosedown-filled jackets have been a staple of manufacturers of ski parkas and other sturdy sports jackets for years. Recently, many designers have recognized the practicality and insulation value of goosedown and have adapted this material to their lines, improving on the funky, sportive parka style. Some of these coats, often full length, are very sophisticated and fashionable. They are, however, still a bit bulky and look best on tallish, slim bodies. The prices of these coats can vary from costly to moderate, depending on the manufacturer.

Fur is a universal favorite. The insulation quality of fine fur is indisputable. Unfortunately, so is the high cost. But a good fur coat is an investment and has a very long life. Many women consider a fur coat a luxury item that should be worn only on special occasions. I disagree. A strong, hearty fur can be worn every day and will stand up to the harshest treatments. My old raccoon coat, for instance, which I bought six years ago, survived my rough handling splendidly until it was stolen last year. Which reminds me of one of the drawbacks of fur. A lot of checkrooms will refuse to accept the responsibility of babysitting for your coat—and that leaves the job to you, which is sometimes inconvenient.

If you are considering the purchase of a fur coat, the end of the winter season is a good time. Most every store has sales, and good bargains in furs abound. But a warning: beware of long-hair furs that shed. Give the coat some gentle tugs before you buy it—if a few hairs come off in your hand, consider another coat. I really cannot say whether a long-hair fur or a flat one would be better for you—it depends on the coat. Long-hair furs have recently been more in vogue, but some designers now seem to be rediscovering the shorter-hair furs. Both kinds of fur will suit all body types if their styling is compatible with the wearer's proportions.

Your coat for evening. The coat you choose for everyday wear for work or important activities should also get you through most of your evenings. A wool coat in a dark color or an attractive fur would be suitable to wear to restaurants and most cocktail and dinner parties, unless these occasions call for formal evening dress. A tailored wool coat will simply not look right over a flowing long dress or pants outfit. Almost all short fur jackets and many below-the-knee and mid-calf-length fur coats will look fine with long dresses, skirts, and dressy pants outfits—another reason that furs are such smart purchases in spite of their hefty price. Any below-the-knee-length coat will look wrong over a mid-calf-length skirt or dress that hangs out by only a few inches. It may pay for you to buy a fur jacket or dressy full-length wool coat if you have many formal evening occasions.

Leisure and cruel winter days. The warmest, most practical winter coverup available is the nylon-covered, goosedown parka. Originally designed for Antarctic explorers, they can keep you warm as toast in below-0-degree temperatures. Unfortunately, they are not very flattering to any body type (although I have never let the fact that I look like a marshmallow stop me from wearing mine to business meetings or even fine restaurants in the dead of winter). No matter what you choose for your main winter coat, I highly rec-

Goosedown vests and parkas are warm and practical for cold winter days.

ommend buying one of these gems as a preparatory measure for the inevitable hard winter days ahead. A warning: down parkas can be addictive. They are so warm, so lightweight, and so practical—you can wear anything underneath them—that other coats just cannot compare. Style and prices vary. They can cost anywhere from $60 to $125, and can be purchased at your local sporting goods store or by mail order from one of the stores that specialize in down-filled items. (My favorite is Eddie Bauer in Seattle, Washington. You can check with information for their toll-free telephone number and ask them to send you a catalog.)

The classic trenchcoat. The most important consideration for choosing a trenchcoat is quality. These coats are true classics and will

be around forever. A well-made trenchcoat can see you through more than ten years of rainy seasons. The Burberry is the ultimate in trenchcoats and is easily worth its fairly hefty price. A great deal of attention is paid to fine details of design (even the heavy wool, button-in lining has an inside pocket). The lined versions come only in khaki color and cost from $300 to $400 depending on the fabric. Unlined Burberrys are priced from $200 to $250 and are available in navy and a lighter shade of blue, green, khaki, and off-white. If these coats are out of your price range, check out the Burberry anyway and note its design details, so that you will have a reference point for comparison as you shop for another brand.

DRESSING FOR THE OCCASION

What exactly is the appropriate dress for a black-tie affair?

What should you wear when an invitation reads "festive dress"?

What is the correct mode of dress for weddings, garden parties, premières, receptions, country club gatherings, the theater?

Although there is plenty of room for many dress options in our everyday lives, specific occasions may limit the range of choices to a certain degree. It is not so much a matter of strictly defined rules of dress—in most cases there are none—as unstated standards of appropriateness. There are certain styles that will make you feel comfortable because you know they are suitable to the surroundings and to the sensibilities of the other guests. You want your dress to be compatible with the general mood and atmosphere of the occasion.

Dressing for the occasion is not as difficult as it may sound. Aside from the specific suggestions I will offer, there is one basic

I'm the sort of person who finds something that she likes very much and will wear it to death. I like a good belt or a bag. I like jewelry, but only the kind of jewelry that means something to me—that's personal.
MAUD ADAMS

guideline that always proves true, and that is that *simplicity is the key to chic.* In any situation, especially if you are in doubt as to the exact mood of a particular event, keep your clothes simple of line, design, and color; make sure that the garments are of fine texture, and you will be one step ahead of the game.

When a special occasion comes around, give some thought to these factors:

☐ The time of the affair (daytime, early evening—5 to 8—or evening)

☐ The location (inside or outdoors, at home or at a restaurant, hotel, or private club)

☐ The purpose of the affair (a charity benefit, an evening in honor of a friend, a family gathering or wedding celebration)

☐ The type of people present (friends and relatives, business associates, acquaintances, or people you don't know at all)

Weather conditions are an obvious consideration for outdoor gatherings. To avoid perspiration stains and discomfort, wear clothes that allow for ultimate coolness in warm weather—either sleeveless or loose in the sleeves and bodice. Dresses are cooler than slacks. If it's chilly or there is a chance that the winds could suddenly blow in, wear a style that will look attractive with an emergency third layer. Decorative shawls often serve this purpose well. Be prepared.

The purpose of the occasion will obviously

influence the general mood of the gathering. Clothing in dark colors, in conservative styles that are fairly plain and simple in line, would be appropriate for serious and somber occasions. Weddings and other gay, festive events call for clothes in fairly light colors and flowing and draped styles, accompanied by festive accessories such as hair combs or flowers pinned in the hair, interesting jewelry, and strappy sandals.

The type of people present should be one of the most important factors in determining how you dress. If the crowd will consist mainly of business associates or visiting heads of state, you would be wise to choose a nicely styled conservative-looking dress or a smart, trim skirt ensemble. An ornamental disco frock would be quite inappropriate.

DAYTIME. Lighter colors are generally more appropriate for formal daytime events—indoors or out—and one solid color or different colors that are very close in tone are the safest. Very bright colors or black are risks. A simple silk dress in beige, lilac, dusty blue, or a very muted rose would see you through most weddings, teas, and afternoon get-togethers. Silk is a good choice because the texture of the fabric will make it look special, and a lustrous, ele-

Style is a recognizable fingerprint.
MARY McFADDEN

What you're wearing can make a big difference in a business meeting. You have to create the image that you want them to see, but still keep your individuality.
SUZY CHAFFEE

gant silk fabric will upgrade any simple design.

Dresses and sophisticated skirt ensembles would be fine for any daytime occasion and are always acceptable. Wearing long gowns in the afternoon is risky. They are too likely to make you appear overdressed—even at the most formal afternoon gatherings. Slacks are also on the borderline. They may be suitable for one occasion and just miss for another. So if there's a doubt in your mind as to their appropriateness for a specific situation, the best idea is to opt for a dress or skirt ensemble.

EARLY EVENING (FIVE TO EIGHT O'CLOCK). The same general information for daytime applies here too, except that as the evening hours approach, the colors can get darker. Black is now acceptable (although probably not the best choice for an outdoor cocktail party in a tropical climate). In warm, balmy climates, light colors and whites are suitable for almost all occasions.

FORMAL EVENINGS. A basic black silk or satin dress in a trim, elegant design will always look right for evening wear. Add a pair of chic strappy sandals, and some expensive-looking jewelry, and you will have a stunning outfit. A beautiful, subtle color such as a deep, rich blue is also quite appropriate. While "black-tie affairs" were once synonymous with conservative-looking clothes, more and more women these days are using their imaginations, and making appearances in smashing fantasy fashions.

Hem length is arbitrary for evening clothes. Anywhere from mid-calf to floor length is perfectly acceptable for any formal evening occasion, though I personally think that street-length dresses, which have recently become very fashionable for evening

When you go into a store, pick out something you like. It doesn't matter if it's 'two-years-ago' antique, or now—it's what appeals to you.
PERRY ELLIS

You don't need a lot of clothes. Just buy very well made clothes that are simple and of very good quality.
FERNANDO SANCHEZ

clothes, are a more contemporary look (though perhaps still not advisable for the more formal black-tie affairs). Very short skirts are definitely out, and slacks are not a good choice for black-tie affairs.

The term *festive dress* seems to be a favorite on invitations these days. It simply means that the general atmosphere will be less formal and the mood more casual than black tie. The safest way to handle this freeform dress request is to keep the tenor of your outfit elegant, the style chic and simple, and add interesting accessories—say, an eye-catching belt or a shiny lamé scarf. A well-styled slacks outfit would be acceptable, but not as safe as a dress. *Festive* means you can be more expressive with your clothes. But do not be fooled. Now more than ever, elegance is the name of the game, and understated chic will always win hands down over far-fetched, costume-y looks.

SHOPPING HINTS

These clothing ideas should help you on your way to creating a wardrobe that will be suitable to your life-style. And they are just a sampling of the possibilities that the fashion of today has to offer. Now that you have a good working knowledge of the basics, and your individual style is beginning to take shape, fashion can begin to be fun rather than a burden. You are still not crazy about going shopping, you say? Don't worry about it, neither am I. Since shopping has been such an integral part of my working life, I hardly consider it a leisure activity. When I do my personal shopping, I like to zip into a store, accomplish my mission, and zip right out again, especially if it's a beautiful day. If you do consider shopping a chore, let me give you a few hints on how you can make it fast, productive, and easy.

1. *Go shopping when you're in the mood and feeling energetic.* Do not dash out at the last minute when you must have something special to wear that very evening, or even the following day. There is no surer way to make mistakes, compromise, or get completely fed up. Keep this in mind for Christmas and birthday gifts too. Don't wait until you *need* something to buy it; you won't find it.

2. *Know the stores that you frequent.* While the smaller boutiques have less of a selection, the merchandise is easier to spot; it is also more likely that you will find a good salesperson who can alert you to special sales, help you with alterations, and understand your needs.

In large department stores learn which departments are most in keeping with your style and budget, and concentrate your efforts there. Breeze through the other departments, but save your major energy burst for your departments.

A quick aside: If you have a small frame, check out the boys' department now and again. There is usually a bargain or two to be had. Boys' sweaters, for example, are much more reasonably priced than the same-quality woman's sweater. Obviously, manufacturers realize that no sensible parent is going to spend too much money on a garment that will soon be outgrown.

3. *Use a process of elimination when you shop.* Since you now know the colors, textures, shapes, and lines that are best for you, let your eye automatically eliminate the others. Don't waste your time on them. That will cut down the options considerably and make shopping much less of a burden. If you spot a sensational pair of pleated trousers, for instance, but you know that the pleated style is not flattering on you, pass them by. Don't say "These are great. I've got to try them on." Unless your body has been through some drastic changes, pleated pants won't look any better on you now than they did the last time. Also, if you spend too much time on them, you'll be too discouraged and too tired to notice or care when you happen across a *real* possibility. To use your time and energy to best advantage, cruise through a store; zero in on a line, color, or texture that strikes your fancy; and move in for a closer check. If it meets all your qualifications, try it on. If it misses on any of these major counts, forget it, and move right along, energy intact.

4. *Don't let the size printed on the label of a garment bother you.* If you're generally a 10 but a 12 fits better, buy it. Since all manufacturers' sizes differ, it is of absolutely no consequence. Don't feel bad because it is a size larger; it's the look and the feel of a garment that count.

5. *When buying a somewhat fitted jacket, keep in mind that you may want to wear it over more than one layer.* Remember to make allowance for this eventuality, as it is easy to forget when you're doing your fall shopping in a lightweight summer frock.

6. If you're on a restricted budget and can afford only one dress for evening, buy it in a darker color. You can change the look with accessories. No one need ever know it's the same dress.

7. *Don't go shopping when you're looking too shabby*—if your hair is in rollers or your jaw is swollen from a visit to the dentist, nothing you put on is going to look great.

8. *It's risky to shop with a friend unless you have a firm sense of what is right for you.* Even the opinions of your most stylish friends may be mirrored in their image—what they like and what they feel comfortable in. What is good for them might not be the best for you. Go shopping alone until you have faith in your wardrobe decisions and your choices come easily. Only then is it possible to profit from shopping with a friend who has good fashion sense—who might spot something that you would pass by.

Husbands and boyfriends don't always make great shopping companions either. They may have a good eye for the finished product but sometimes can't judge individual components. Hence their response to a certain item might be less enthusiastic than you had hoped for and you may begin to doubt your choice.

Once you really understand your body and its proportions you will almost never be disappointed in a purchase. But you have to try things on and take a good look at yourself. Just because something's in fashion doesn't mean it's right for you.
POLLY MELLEN

If you're still walking around in 1979 wanting to look like Brigitte Bardot, it's time for a little introspection. People should never stop growing, learning, and experiencing.
WILLI SMITH

The cover of the January 1979 issue of *Vogue* was emblazoned with bold red letters declaring BE GOOD TO YOURSELF. This, indeed, is an important step in enjoying fashion and, I might add, to enjoying life. The preceding chapters have provided you with information on what makes fashion work. The rest has to come from you—how you feel about yourself and the way you treat yourself. Remember that good fashion is built not only on basic fashion principles but on a positive attitude and an understanding of your strongest points. The ability to make the most of what you have will follow.

In *Womanstyle* I have tried to describe the many fashion alternatives currently available and to assist you in finding the style that suits you best—a style that will not only complement your body type but will let who you are shine through. Today, more than ever before, we are free to express our individuality. We are living in the best, that is, the freest, most creative time yet for fashion. The blue-jeaned "freedom" of the 60s and early 70s actually produced its own kind of uniformity, and while we may still choose to wear jeans today, we do not feel compelled to wear them. They are no longer the emblematic style of dress they once were. The 80s promise something a lot more satisfying: the freedom to dress up again, to be imaginative and glamorous, and to truly have fun with fashion.

INDEX